TAKE TIME
TO SMELL THE
DANDELIONS

TAKE TIME TO SMELL THE DANDELIONS

Karla C. Erickson

Bookcraft
Salt Lake City,
Utah

Library of Congress Catalog Card Number: 78-75283
ISBN 0-88494-360-7

2nd Printing, 1979

Lithographed in the United States of America
PUBLISHERS PRESS
Salt Lake City, Utah

To Barry,
my husband, friend, and editor

Many times
    A dandelion
Is a weed
    In the green, grassy sod

But a dandelion
    Is a flower divine
In the hands
    Of a child of God.

Contents

Preface

The majority of you who read this book will be parents who are busy raising families, busy earning livings, busy performing church callings, and busy being active in your communities.

This book has been written for *you*. It is written in a fast-moving style so that you might have the time to fit it into your hectic schedule and to actually read it. Then while you are accomplishing necessary daily tasks, you can be thinking about some of these ideas and adjusting them to your individual family needs.

I have shared many true-to-life examples with you. These examples are presented concisely, without sugar-coating. It is hoped that you will here find some ideas which can help you achieve the kind of home most parents dream about but never get around to actually creating because they fail to "take the time to smell the dandelions."

Evaluate and Dream

One warm, sunny summer afternoon when our daughter was only three, I was sitting on our front porch reading the newspaper. She came running towards me, her little chubby legs carrying her as fast as they could. With her dark brown eyes sparkling, she handed me a bunch of bright yellow dandelions. I took them gently, told her they were pretty and hugged her for a special thanks. Then I laid them beside me and started to pick up the newspaper to resume my reading.

"Smell them, Mommy," she pleaded.

So I picked them up again and smelled them. A broad smile covered her cherub face and then I understood the true value of those dandelions — no longer were they just weeds on my lawn. She scurried off to some other adventure, but I remained sitting and holding the dandelions. "How many other times had I neglected to smell the dandelions?" I thought to myself. "How many other moments which I could have shared with the children or my husband had I casually laid aside, not realizing the true value of those fragile moments?"

Those dandelions seemed to tell me that perhaps I had missed many special moments.

Since that day, Barry and I have incorporated the use of three simple steps to help us to "smell the dandelions" while raising our children. These steps are:

1. Evaluate
2. Dream
3. Take action

Take time to seriously evaluate the attitudes in your home. Do you find an electric feeling of good cheer, happiness and contentment, or a feeling of unconcern for one another and discontent, with everyone going his own way? Do your children love and respect you or are they allowed to speak rudely to you and to each other? Does the family work together to keep the home orderly, both in appearance and atmosphere, or do mother and father have to constantly nag to get help from family members?

After this kind of preliminary evaluation, take time to dream. Dream about the kind of home you would like. Dream about being a good parent and dream about the kind of children you want.

Now comes the hard part — take some action! If your dreams are exciting and enticing, but your present home situation doesn't measure up, find the means to make your dreams come true.

Before we had any children, I dreamed of the way our children would feel about Barry and me. There would be mutual respect and a peaceful feeling. Yet the first time our two-year-old talked back to us with a very strong no, I could see that the fulfillment of dreams doesn't just happen. That doesn't mean dreams can't be made to come true, but I knew it would take real work to make my dreams come true.

Often we need to use clever ways to put across important ideas. One example I have used to instill in our children admiration for their father is to say, "Go tell your *neat* Daddy . . ." They seem to get the intended message. I have even used this idea when referring to myself. When I offer them a treat I often say, "Now what do you tell your *neat* Mom?" I slip the *neat* into the sentence ever so lightly, but it works! You can use the same idea when talking about brothers and sisters, also.

Take the time as parents to share your good feelings about your mate. If the wife fixes a good meal, how appropriate it is to have the husband tell the children how much he appreciates having a wife who is a good cook. He can remind the boys to find a wife who can cook well and he can remind his daughters to be sure and learn the talent their mother has. Much good results when parents build spouse esteem in the presence of their children.

Parents need to be united in teaching the children that what one parent wants for the family, the other parent wants also. One steadfast rule in our home is that no one can call the parents disrespectful names. Often a child will not attempt to name-call if he knows that his parents firmly agree on such matters and that he will have to face both parents when he is disobedient.

Take the time to evaluate the feelings you have about your children. Do you enjoy their company or do they "drive you up a wall"? If you do not enjoy the company of your children, possibly it is because neither you nor your child is aware of the good times which a parent and child can share.

For example, when our children were young and I was swamped with diapers and feeding times, I sometimes resented the fact that I had no time to myself. I was so busy caring for the babies that I was not relaxing with them or inviting myself into their magical worlds of adventure.

One afternoon I sat on the floor with them. At first all I could see were crumbs on the floor and marks on the wall boards, but gradually my eyes began to open. I was intrigued! I put my typewriter on the coffee table, sat on the floor, and typed an article about how once my husband and I were just two, but now we were five. It was the first article I sent out for publication — and it sold. These little people whom I had been caring for, but not living with, were a catalyst for a new adventure. No matter how much time I was giving to make their lives better, they were giving much more to enrich my life! I started to share my feelings with them. When I received the check for my article, I gathered them around me, waved the envelope before them, and shared my uninhibited enthusiasm!

In order to have the time to share moments with young children, a mother has to schedule her time much as a professional person has to schedule his. The professional has to rise fairly early and prepare for the day. Once at work, a certain amount of time is usually spent doing routine tasks, whether it is going through mail or outlining the day's schedule. The mother should do likewise and allow herself only a scheduled amount of time each day to do the necessary tasks of straightening the house, washing and ironing the clothes, and preparing meals.

After several weeks of constant practice in such scheduling, a habit is formed and success seems much closer. After completing the necessities, you can do what is important to you, and of course this will vary with each individual. But if a mother can accomplish something each day which she terms important, that day is a success.

During the initial part of evaluating, you will come to realize what is important to you. You will get to know yourself better, because you will need to recognize what you want most out of life. Sometimes it might be painful to admit that you do not really enjoy your little children. But once you recognize your needs and desires, when you start to dream, many of the problems have a way of working themselves out.

For example, when Barry and I were first married, a clean house was very important to me. I wanted everything to sparkle. In fact, I went from room to room and stood in the doorway and admired how nice each room looked. Then (it seemed to happen all of a sudden) I had three little people who kept messing up my clean rooms. During my evaluation, I recognized that a clean house was important to me. During my dreaming step, however, I came to realize what was *most* important to me.

I had always wanted a home where our children could feel relaxed and could enjoy the company of each other. I realized that I was expecting them to eat without spilling, play without cluttering, and crawl without getting dirty. My desires for a perfect house and spotless children did not coincide with my dreams of a happy and contented family, so I had to make the decision — which was most important to me? My house would last a lifetime possibly, but my children could be with me for eternity. That answered my question. So of course the next step was to take action and make my dreams a reality.

I could not fully relinquish a straight and orderly home, however, so I confronted the children with my desires. I told them that I liked a clean house and that I *needed* their help in keeping our home straight — believe it or not, they became my helpers. Our house still had a certain amount of clutter and mess during their learning stages, but we seemed to be working together more for a common goal. Again and again I have reflected upon that decision, that my children were more important than a clean house.

And now, after living with these little people for nine years, I feel even better about the decision. They agree that they also like a straight home, and so they are willing to work with me to keep it clean. Everything doesn't sparkle all the time in our home, but there are some children's eyes which do.

Another part of evaluating can be in the area of habits. What habits are you and your children forming this very day? Do you arise early or do you sleep in? Do the children have specific required chores or are the tasks done haphazardly? Are your mealtimes and bedtimes consistent or erratic?

Since we are forming habits every day, it is imperative that we sit down and dream about the habits we want our families to form. Consider your needs as parents. Earlier I mentioned my need to have a straight home. If the mother feels that this is important, she should train her children to help with the housework. If she assigns them chores, she should supervise them until they know how to accomplish the work. When they have learned the techniques, however, let them handle the job. Children must learn to do their jobs just as we had to learn to do ours. Do you remember when a simple thing like tying your shoelaces was difficult?

I think of my newly married friend who called her mother to ask her how to make jello. "Mom, you always did everything and I never had to learn," she said. Her poor mother was horrified! "If I had it to do over again," she said, "I would not have been so efficient. I would have given the children the opportunity to learn for themselves."

I was fortunate to have a very wise mother. Although I was eager to learn how to cook, she was very uncomfortable with me in the kitchen. I was not disciplined and would not use measuring utensils. I was truly an "uninhibited cook." After she had spent time teaching me certain techniques, she realized that no matter how hard she tried, she could never make a conventional cook out of me. So she left me alone in her kitchen and let me experiment with new ideas and recipes, while she went shopping or visiting. Her only word of caution was that I must clean everything up when I was finished. I never did fully appreciate her doing this until I had little ones in *my* kitchen. Could I have made messes like they do? Of course, my children are still too young to be left alone to cook, but thanks to my mother's example, I now have enough wisdom to include them in my baking moments and to let them spill ingredients or eat cookie dough without scolding. In fact, the kitchen has become one of our favorite places in our home!

So while teaching the children to be independent, I was also making it a habit to include my children in my routine activities. We can't just hope our children will develop good habits; we must dream of the habits we want them to form and then create situations that will reinforce the desired action.

One habit I have tried to form is that of treating my children kindly. Children can be our best friends. They can help us see the flowers of life. When one of your children presents you with a handful of dandelions, take the time to smell them. Then find a vase or a little glass and give those "flowers" a place of honor in your kitchen.

One easy way to let your children know you respect their ideas and opinions is to invite them into your world. If you are preparing to go out to dinner with your husband, and your children walk into your bedroom, ask them for an opinion on how you look. Ask them if they like your outfit. Children are honest and they can be your best critics.

Once my perceptive little son came into my bedroom as I was getting ready to go out for the evening. "How do I look?" I asked him.

"Well, Mom, I don't want to make you feel bad, but I like the other blouse better." I took his advice, and by golly, he was right. I felt great the entire evening. And my son felt great too, because he knew I valued his judgment.

A devastating feeling in the heart of a child is to know he has such efficient parents that there is no real need for him in the family. Let your children know they are needed by you. When you get in a bind, call upon your children for help, then express your gratefulness to them for helping you out of a dilemma. This idea was vividly illustrated in our own family. I was scheduled to give a program at the League of Utah Writers, Salt Lake Chapter. I had an artist lined up to do some pictures of my subject material and I thought all was organized. Four days before the event, the artist called to say it was impossible for her to do the work. I was frantic! I am not an artist so I was at my wit's end.

Then I thought of my children, who love to draw and color. The program included some children's songs about a little green caterpillar and some butterflies and an oak tree. I explained my dilemma to the kids and asked if they would do my art work. They excitedly said they would help me, so we headed to the store and bought paints and poster paper. They worked for hours, especially our oldest who was seven at the time. He even got up early before school to put some finishing touches on the pictures.

The evening I left to give my program, all three children and Barry were at the door wishing me good luck. "I sure hope they like our pictures," Jeff called. "Wake us up and tell us when you get home." With a send-off like that, how could I fail? And by the way, the pictures were one of the highlights of the program.

That experience taught me an invaluable lesson. Share your talents and hobbies with your family. Involve them in what you are doing. Let them know of your successes and your dis-appointments. Not only will this bring you closer as family members, but you will open their eyes to the joys of having varied interests.

Most adults feel that their talents and hobbies are much too advanced for children. But if each of us will do some diligent soul-searching, I believe we can include our children in our interests. Writing is not exactly a child's hobby, but through sharing your articles with them, you can get a fresh reaction to your ideas. My family knows that it is important to me to spend time writing because I have told them so. But they have not been excluded.

Barry, who has become my right-hand editor, has great talent at picking out my detail errors. I read the articles to my children to see if they think the articles are interesting.

By sharing our feelings about our hobbies and interests, we make it much easier for our children to likewise share their feelings, dreams and disappointments with us. Sometimes their dreams seem outlandish. But when we have made it a habit to listen to them chatter about going to the moon, or being a cheerleader for the Dallas Cowboys football team, we really get to know these little people we are supposed to know so well. If our children know we have entrusted them with our dreams and aspirations, they are much more willing to share their dreams with us. It is important for a parent to know what his child talks about when there is nothing to talk about.

Another good habit to form is that of making use of those moments when you and your children can quietly chat. Some of our family's favorite moments occur when we are all crowded together on one of our beds talking about anything which comes to our minds. By making use of these not-too-often occasions, Barry and I have come to know of some of the dreams our children have, and it gives our family a chance to dream together. Whether we talk about the dog we are going to get someday or about the vacation we want to take as a family to Hawaii, we have learned to enjoy the companionship of each other. Not all of our talk is about the dreams each of us has; we also discuss current situations. But I'll never forget what my brother told me: To always have a dream in my head because someday it might come true if I wanted it badly enough.

I hope some of the ideas in the following chapters will give you help in achieving your dreams concerning your family life. Since every family is different, my ideas and those of other people might not be what your home needs. But possibly these ideas can open the way to other ideas which you will be able to use, thus helping you to realize your dreams in your home and family life.

Do Your Children Fight?

Do your children fight? If you can answer yes to this question, you are not alone. What gets into our kids? All of a sudden they are calling each other names like "dummy" or "do-do bird," and even "idiot" slips into their vocabularies. It seems that they go in stages from name-calling to not sharing with each other. Some weeks are pretty good, but then everything breaks loose and they act like they can't stand each other.

My first reaction is to vocally scold and tell them, "We don't talk like that in our home." But that carries little weight. We have found something, however, which works and is fun for the entire family.

When our children were very young, they were being extremely selfish with each other. Since they were close in age to one another, they battled over which toy was whose. One evening the entire family, armed with scissors, glue and colored paper, gathered around the table. The kids were excited about being cowboys and a cowgirl, so we cut out three cowboy guns. Then we wrote *sharing* in the middle of each gun and taped them to the kitchen door where they would be seen.

We told the kids the rules. Every time one of them shared with another, he could put a star on his gun. Each time one of them was selfish with a toy, he lost a star. Only Mom or Dad could hand out the stars or take away the stars. I wrapped up three surprises and put them on the kitchen counter. (Just seeing those packages every day seemed to spur them on!) At the end of a week the one with the most stars would win the contest, and could pick the first prize. The one who came in second was allowed to pick the second prize. The third one had to take what was left.

It might not sound like much of a contest, but did it ever work! They were so eager to share everything they had that I found myself laughing inside and out as they ran to claim another star. When the youngest slipped behind, the older children took him into their rooms and encouraged him to share with them. There were no rules on what they could share — snacks, toys, books, or crayons. The decision was theirs.

In only a week's time, this exciting contest lifted them out of their ugly mood of being selfish. Barry and I could have told them inspiring stories and scolded them for a week, but how much better it is for them to experience the rewards of being generous and kind rather than selfish and mean.

Through the years we have found, by using contests, that the problems of fighting and arguing are put into the hands of the children for solution, without parental nagging and correcting. We do have to uphold the rules which are set, but that is much more pleasant than hollering at the kids.

When we had the first contest, I was concerned that the child who won the contest would feel slighted if the other children also won a prize. But the fact that the winner could be the first to choose a prize was reward enough. Whatever the problem, create the kind of contest best suited for your family and formulate the rules which are best for you.

Another contest tackled the problem of children talking disrespectfully to each other. (We use contests only when there is a need, otherwise they become too common.) The kids had started jeering at each other and they were treating each other unkindly. During family home evening we took three huge pieces of white paper and cut out silhouettes of heads about twice the size of each child's. Then each child colored a head to look like himself. For our daughter, we added pigtails at the side. We then hung the pictures on the kitchen door. I wrapped three prizes in bright paper and bows, wrote each child's name on one, and put them on the counter. Just seeing those packages got them excited.

The rules were simple. Every time they said something nice, they could have a star. To win the prize with their name on, they had to have stars completely around the head. Every time one said something unkind, Barry or I removed a star from that person's silhouette. Bright and early the next morning the kids were up greeting each other with hugs and asking how they had slept. They were great to thank me for breakfast too. Every one of us had a super day! A good feeling in our home was the happy result.

Our little daughter sat at the counter as I was preparing dinner. "Gosh, Mom," she said, "you haven't even been mad at us today. These contests make you a better Mom too." I had to laugh and agree with her. How could a mom possibly get angry at kids who were so nice?

The good resulting from the contest wasn't confined to our family. Jeff came home from school excited. "Our contest sure works, Mom," he said. "In school a friend sits right behind me, and every day he pokes me in the back and asks if he can borrow my eraser. Every other day I didn't want to give him my eraser, but I said, 'Well, okay.' But today I was in the habit of saying nice things and when he poked me and asked for my eraser, I said, 'Sure! You can use it any time.' He looked really happy."

Prizes for our contests are kept inexpensive. I watch in the stores for little ten-cent presents, such as pencils, erasers, bracelets and rings. We feel that the most important prize should be the good feeling that improved behavior brings to the home.

Be sure to point out to the kids the difference in the home atmosphere. Talk about it as a family. Most children seem to like a peaceful setting, so let them know that they can be the ones to help the home be the way they want it to be.

Some of the contests you might want to consider are:
Sharing week
Talking nicely to each other week
Doing daily chores
Reading good books

Sharing with friends and neighbors

Doing good deeds for relatives

Another activity which promotes involvement is to have a secret pal within the family. We put everyone's name into a hat, then each person chooses a name. During the week each family member is to do at least one good thing for his secret pal each day. They can secretly make beds for each other, do their pal's daily chores, draw them a pretty picture, put a treat on their bed for after school or many other things. Even if the identity of a pal is discovered, the activity continues for a whole week. Then at family home evening, the secret pals are openly disclosed and each one gives his secret pal something special. (Here again, keep the gifts simple.)

This activity has brought good feelings into our home because every member is thinking about someone else and wanting to do something for him. Every member of the family is a winner because we grow closer together and we get to know that feeling of doing good things for those we should love.

The secret of success in these family contests and activities is that the parents are excited. The parents' enthusiasm is contagious. I believe that we can get our families to do just about anything if we are enthusiastic. "Nothing great was ever accomplished without enthusiasm." I think that quote from Emerson has sometimes pushed me ahead when it would have been easier to sit back and watch.

A Friend Is a Good Thing

Our children — their friends — our home! I sometimes find it difficult to really "love and adore" all of the little friends who come into our home with our children. Maybe it's because I don't enjoy the soda crackers spread across the kitchen when my children are generous with snacks. Maybe it's the feeling of being invaded. Maybe it's because I would sometimes like to talk to my children without an audience.

My brother, who lives in the country, recently mentioned that he can almost handpick the friends who play with his children. His children telephone their friends and invite them over to play. But when you live in town, it is not quite so easy to pick the time and the place. The neighborhood children can come at the most unexpected moments — and they do! Most mothers have probably experienced a neighborhood child running into her home shouting that little Johnny is throwing dirt at him. It takes a clever mom to solve that problem, especially if she's standing in the shower!

How do you keep friends — your children's friends — a good thing instead of a headache? One summer I found myself in a real dilemma. I had always liked to fix snacks for the children, but I soon came to realize that our home was the most popular one on the block as soon as the brownies came out of the oven. Kids from blocks away seemed to pick up the aroma of warm brownies. As I overheard little friends whisper to my children, "Go ask your mom for some more brownies," I started to steam inside. My first reaction was to stop making treats. I even suggested to Barry that we move to the country. But thank goodness for a little wisdom! It sometimes seems to slip out of heaven just at a time when I might foul up my life!

I called all of the children together, ours and the neighbors'. "Okay, kids," I said, as we all sat Indian-style on the front lawn. "I'm not going to be able to make it through the summer if we don't have a few rules to go by. Number one, I like you kids. I like to give you treats because I know you like them. But I don't like to have you beg for them. If I make a treat and want to surprise you, I will. But if anyone begs for a treat, *no one* gets any. Does everyone understand?" All of the little heads nodded.

"Rule number two," I continued. "I consider this house to be the Ericksons'. I like to have you come in and play, but unless you are invited to come in, please don't run into my home unless there is an emergency. That even includes using the bathroom. Everyone run to your own home to use the bathroom — unless it is an emergency! Okay?" Again their little heads nodded.

I felt as though a hundred pounds of weight had just been lifted from me. I had been honest with them in telling them my feelings. And just telling them that I liked them made me look at each one and realize that I really did like them. Oh, the entire summer wasn't perfect, but I know it was a lot better than if I had just fumed inside every time they wanted a treat or had to go to the bathroom.

Now, as I look back, I am embarrassed that these incidental things could upset my life. When I was facing a predicament for the first time, I panicked because I didn't know that those moments would not last forever. Now our children are older and so are their friends. Age has dissolved many of the previous problems, but added new ones. Knowing from experience that many problems will not last forever makes me less likely to overreact to the situation.

In learning to love your children's friends, the best policy is to be honest with them. If your whole family is engaged in an activity when a little friend comes to play, politely tell him that the family is busy just now. Of course, if the children beat you to the door, they might want to play with the friend more than with the family.

One clever mother used this idea. She drew a picture of a bee, large enough that it could be seen from a block away. She then introduced her children to the bee. "This is a new friend," she told them. "When we are busy coloring or doing scrapbooks, we will put the bee on our door with this little poem:

Sorry kids, we're busy as bees.
Come back later, if you please.

Your little friends will know when they see the bee that you are busy with your family and that you can play later." Her comment after one month with the bee was: "Boy! Does this idea ever work!"

Sometimes if we plan moments with our children, we can become distraught when a friend ruins the experience. A "busy bee" idea can easily solve the problem, and no one will have hurt feelings.

Learning to love "little people" is sometimes as difficult as learning to love "big people." With the myriad friends our children bring through our doors, it has sometimes been a challenge to find something lovable about each one of them. Sometimes I let a runny nose or dirty hands hold me back from giving a little friend a hug. I learned that all it takes is a handkerchief, soap, and a little time and concern to break the barriers. It's not the nose or hands I should be most concerned with; it's reaching out to their hearts to start a friendship.

The first step in learning to love our children's friends is to pick out something about them which we truly do like — even if it's nothing more than a pair of big brown eyes. Looking for one good trait usually leads to the discovery of even more good traits.

Loving the friends of our children can benefit us and our children. Our daughter is very lucky because she has a girl friend who is just like a sister. They spend hours together. Once while they were pretending to be cheerleaders for the Dallas Cowboys, they called for me to come and see their cheer. As I sat on the floor watching them jump up and down and giggle and laugh, my thoughts drifted back to my cheerleading days in high school. Maybe it was the emotion of recalling fond memories or just the joy of seeing my little girl so happy and carefree. Whatever the reason, I grabbed the two of them and hugged them hard. "I love you girls," I told them.

Some time later that same day, I noticed Cori wasn't her usual cheerful self. I put my arm around her shoulders and asked what was bothering her. Tears came to her eyes as she said, "Oh, Mom, I bet you love Cindy more than me."

I was startled. What had brought this on? The more we talked, the more I realized that when I had hugged the two girls and told them I loved them, my little girl felt that I loved her friend more than I did her. My first reaction was to tell her that she was silly for thinking such a thought. But I held my tongue and thought for just a minute.

"I do love Cindy," I told her. "But one of the main reasons I love Cindy is that you love her and she is your friend."

I proceeded to tell Cori how much I loved having her for my daughter and that no one could ever take her place. We even talked about that age-old problem of letting jealousy slip into our lives and ruin some of the joys of life. I told her that I, too, had felt similar feelings when I was growing up. I told her that even now I have to watch myself so that I don't get jealous of my friends when something good happens to them. It was a perfect time to let her know that if we feel good about ourselves, when good things happen to our friends, we will be able to share their joy. And that's what having friends is all about. I'm sure the entire message wasn't absorbed, because that is a lesson which sometimes takes a lifetime to understand.

Little children benefit from their friends in many ways. When they have to learn to obey the household rules in their friends' homes, they are learning to respect other people. Eventually that simple concept might have a direct bearing on how they, as adults, obey the rules of our country and city. Another benefit is the opportunity for the child to observe different life-styles. His ideas on how a home can be managed will be broadened.

Just the other afternoon our oldest son brought three of his boyfriends home. They were ravenous and so excited to see a pan full of chocolate chip bars. It was the first time I had used the recipe and I wanted to know their reactions. So I had them sit at the counter and told them I wanted to hear the first words that popped into their minds when they tasted the brownies. They hooted! I cut four large squares and put them on separate plates.

"Okay," I told them, "take a big bite and let me know what you think."

Luckily they liked the new recipe and they eagerly blurted out, "Great!" "Fantastic!" "Mm-m-m-m," and "Can I have another?"

We were all laughing. They started talking about school and reports that were due. They talked about things they had done that day at school. Then they started telling jokes. One of the boys started to tell a joke which I sensed was not one of which I really approved.

"Okay, you guys," I said. "You know how upset moms get when they hear words they don't like and when they hear jokes that aren't very nice. Who'll keep making the treats if you upset me?"

They laughed and I laughed, yet they got the point. They changed the subject.

My children know which words I expect them not to use; and what I expect of my children, I expect of their friends. Maybe the friends don't always agree, but they have surely gone out of their way to do what I like.

I recall when our children were very young and had their friends over. I didn't want to hurt feelings, so sometimes I let the friends do what I wouldn't let my own children do — like jumping over the couch. I found myself getting upset with my children because of what their friends were doing. Thank heaven for a good neighbor who called one afternoon and gave me this advice: "Now you make sure my son obeys your house rules. I want you to correct him if he does wrong. You are not only helping my boy when you do this, but you are helping me."

Her advice gave me the self-confidence I needed to enforce my own house rules. I realized that the children were happier knowing exactly what they could and could not do. My neighbor's advice made me recall the strong conviction I held as a school-teacher — students are much happier and more secure if they know the rules and know that they are expected to obey them. I realized that my children and their friends were just like a new classroom of students — they needed rules that would be enforced.

Peers are important and necessary in a child's life. Are you going to open your doors and let their friends into your family life or are you going to try and keep them out-of-doors?

One mother of three teenage boys impressed me with her philosophy. She said that as her boys were growing up, she recognized that sometimes their peers had more influence on her sons' actions than she did. She decided that the best plan would be to include the friends in the family and thus keep abreast of what was going on. She wanted to know what shows they were seeing, which girls they were dating, and what their favorite pastimes included. In order to do this, she had to open her doors and welcome her sons' friends. She felt it was much wiser to buy pizzas, chips and other "teenage foods" and let the kids have a home to be in, rather than give her sons money to go to movies or other places where she had no control over the environment.

"That way," she said, "you might not have full control over what your children are doing, but you do have some. It takes money and energy to have the kids around a lot of the time, but I feel my boys are worth the price I must pay."

Sometimes when our children bring several friends into our home, I find myself noticing the clutter and crumbs which they leave behind. When I stopped expecting the kids to maintain spotless areas where they ate and uncluttered rooms where they played, I became a happier mother. I had not changed their behavior, but I had altered my own. My rule is, You can have the house straight until 3:00 P.M., then it's time to forget the house.

Not only do I like to be waiting for the children when they come home from school, I also like to have a snack waiting for them and their friends. That is one way I can let them know that I have been anticipating their coming home and that I am excited to see them. Try the approach, "I knew you were coming so I baked a cake." Kids love to know they are welcome and wanted. Some of the favorite recipes of our kids and their friends are included in this chapter.

Jeff's Peanut Butter Brownies

2 cubes margarine
2 cups brown sugar
2 eggs
2 cups flour
2 cups quick oatmeal

Mix all ingredients in the order given and then pat into a cookie sheet which has sides. Bake for 22 minutes at 350°. Remove from the oven, spread with creamy peanut butter, and top with chocolate icing. While still warm, cut into squares and let cool.

Indian Bread

1 cup water
4 tsps. baking powder
1 tsp. salt
2 1/2 to 3 cups flour

Combine ingredients. Knead until smooth and then roll out to 1/4-inch thickness. Cut into squares and cook in hot oil until brown. Remove from oil and let drain on paper towels. Salt to taste, if desired. Serve while warm.

Carameled Popcorn

1 pound package brown sugar
1 cup white corn syrup
1 cube butter
1 can sweetened condensed milk (14 oz.)
  [popped popcorn (about three batches)]

Combine sugar and syrup. Stir until it boils. Add the butter; stir until butter melts and mixture boils. Add the milk gradually. Cook to the softball stage. Spread over popcorn and mix to coat.

Butter Brittles
(Recipe supplied by Gwen Remund)

Soda crackers
1 cup butter (do not use margarine)
1 cup brown sugar
6 oz. package chocolate chips
chopped nuts

Break enough soda crackers (just squeeze them with your hands) to cover the bottom of a jelly roll pan.

Combine butter and sugar; boil for 2 to 2 1/2 minutes. Spread butter mixture over the crackers and put into oven for 5 minutes at 400°. (The crackers should bubble up and float.)

Remove from oven. Spread chocolate chips evenly and let melt over cracker mixture. Top with chopped nuts. Let cool before cutting into squares.

Some other favorite treats include: apples, oranges, carrots, popcorn, popped wheat, dried fruit (including fruit leather).

When I don't have fresh fruit to make fruit leather, I use a bottle of my home-canned fruit and drain off the juice. I blend the fruit, spread it over plastic wrap and let it dry in the sun. During winter I just leave the fruit in front of a sunny window — it takes about two days to dry.

These are just a few of the recipes and ideas which I use to say welcome to the children when they get home from school. But much more important than the treat they get is the greeting I give them. Sometimes I still have to remind myself that my child's friend can be a good thing. Having friends gives our children the opportunity to learn the rules of friendship. It teaches them to care for someone and to trust someone. If a child can learn to be a good friend, he will become a better person.

Are Your Mornings a Mess?

Before our children reached school age, I would overhear mothers talking about their horrible mornings trying to get the kids out the door. Some of those children would leave crying, some would leave feeling angry, and some would leave having had Cheerios for breakfast because they got up too late for a hot meal.

I was determined that our mornings would not be like that! (You know how you are when you are young and idealistic.)

By the time our second child started school, I knew whereof these mothers spoke. Sometimes our little daughter would stand in front of her closet and say she had nothing to wear to school. Everything I suggested was wrong and she'd burst into tears. I panicked. I had to get breakfast, write out the lunch money checks, and there she stood crying. That was when I took action with some new rules.

Every night the children had to lay on their beds the clothes they wanted to wear to school the next morning. That way, if something was torn or had a button off, I had the time to fix it. They also put out the socks and shoes they wanted to wear. Not only was it a good learning experience on how to get organized, but it taught them to make decisions on matching and coordinating their clothes. My boys didn't have much of a problem because most things go with levis, and those were the only pants they wanted to wear. But Cori had to learn why some plaids and polka dots just don't go together. So the first part of the dilemma was solved.

The second decision was what time they had to be in bed so they would be fully rested at an early hour in the morning. If they started at 8:00 P.M., brushing teeth and putting out their clothes, we knew they could be settled by 8:30 — so 8:30 became the bedtime hour.

One morning I tried an experiment. Instead of waking them vocally, I turned on some music as soon as I was up and then began preparing breakfast. They knew it was time to get up; they made their beds, got dressed in the outfits which were already laid out, and we were off to a good start. The music seemed to put them in a good mood. Even though the breakfast menu didn't please everyone, few negative comments were heard. As they left happily for school that morning, I resolved to start each day like that.

I feel a heavy responsibility to prepare a good nourishing breakfast for the day's start. As I mentioned, the children don't always love what I fix (though I try to serve their favorite dishes equally), but they realize they must eat a good breakfast.

Vary the menus. Don't have pancakes five mornings in a row. There are a variety of ways to fix eggs: scrambled, hard-boiled, fried, poached, or in an omelet. French toast is another way of including eggs. There are several kinds of cooked cereals, some of them requiring only the addition of boiling water.

Once in a while, take the time to make fresh muffins or biscuits. Ask other mothers what they fix for breakfast, and you will probably find new recipes to use. By using fresh new ideas and taking pride in knowing you are starting your children's day right, breakfast time can become enjoyable. Sometimes the way a mother prepares her meals tells her children that either they are loved and worth the effort, or they are just one big bother!

Thank goodness for mornings! Every day it is a chance to start anew. The attitudes children have when they walk out the door tell you whether they are facing the new day with enthusiasm or with dread.

Make sure that you pray together as a family every morning. I once heard someone ask, "How can you send your little ones out into the world each morning without a prayer for them?" That took on great meaning to me. I was dedicated to sending my children off with a good breakfast; but how important it is to also send them off with a prayer in their hearts.

One young mother was worried that her children were not getting enough spiritual guidance at school. They didn't live around other children of their faith. In fact, very few children of their faith attended the school. So she decided to read them a story each morning before they went to school. Usually she chose an inspiring story of one of the prophets. She kept the stories short and to the point, then they knelt as a family for family prayer. Her comment was: "Not only are the children leaving the home with good thoughts in their minds, but my husband and I are starting each day with inspiring thoughts. Our whole family is benefiting."

Another young mother adds: "The success of my day begins the night before, when I plan my schedule as much as possible. It helps to let my kids know what I am planning to do tomorrow. I also ask for their ideas of what they would like to do."

Take the last fifteen minutes of each evening to do a quick pickup in the house. One clever mother even sets her breakfast table the night before so that she has one jump on the morning. With a straight home, clothes on the bed, the table set, and all of the kids asleep early the night before, how could the morning go wrong?

Of course, everything doesn't always go that smoothly. But with some effort, your mornings will improve.

One successful idea I have tried is to stand at the front door as the children leave for school. Each one receives a good-bye kiss and usually the last words they hear from me are: "Have a good day! I sure do love you!"

That starts my day off right. I know that if I should be taken during the day and my children were never to see me again, the last words they would have heard me say are words I would want them to always remember.

Is Bedtime a Bad Time?

When our three children were ages five, four, and two, Barry and I had a hard time getting them to bed. The biggest problem was that we had not completely decided *when* they should go to bed. If they went to bed at 8:00 P.M. or 9:00 P.M. we didn't really mind. They weren't in school so we didn't feel any pressure because we knew they could sleep in. But when they went to bed at a late hour we missed having time alone. Overall, our schedule wasn't very organized.

Barry and I went on a three-day trip while my parents took care of the kids at our home. When we came home, the first thing my folks said was: "We've got the kids on a schedule for going to bed. Now stick to it. They are expected to be in bed by 8:00 P.M."

We couldn't believe the first night home. We started getting them ready for bed at 7:30 and they were in bed at 8:00. The next night was the same and we liked the feeling. We finally had an organized schedule.

Being young parents, we had failed at setting some standard rules. I can't say why, unless perhaps we expected the children to rebel. But we discovered that children thrive on standard rules. They are secure in knowing what is expected of them. That episode made us more confident to initiate and enforce other rules which would make our home life better. From that day forward, we have had no trouble with the hour for bedtime.

We have noticed, however, that our oldest child doesn't seem to require as much rest as the others. Therefore, we allow him to leave a light on and read for awhile, but he must stay in bed.

One mother says that when bedtime is exciting, it can be the best time of day. She describes her tactics:

"When the word *bedtime* is heard, children scramble to get bathed, dressed in pajamas, and teeth brushed so the festivities can begin. When everyone is ready, we gather together on a comfortable floor somewhere and decide what game to play. The kids love 'tickle-bee' the best. I am the tickle-bee and we have a designated area in which we can run. I chase after them and when I catch one, he gets tickled. Sounds crazy, but they love it. As a matter of fact, they start talking about it in the morning and throughout the day. When the tickle-bee is after them, they get a certain look in their eyes that I wouldn't trade for anything.

"Sometimes they choose to do exercises. Their father and I join in and the whole family gets their physical workout for the day.

"After games or exercises each child picks out a story he wants read. We snuggle together on the floor and read. After reading the stories, their father or I tell a scripture story, since we like to end our day spiritually. Next comes prayers and a loving tuck into bed."

But that is not the end of their festivities. She continues: "I go to each child to find out what was the best thing that happened to him during the day so I can record it in his journal. The final curtain comes when I turn out their bedroom lights and stand in the hall sorting the clothes for tomorrow's washing. While I'm sorting, we're all talking quietly to each other. (Kids are so cooperative and talkative when it comes to staying awake a few minutes more!)

"Except for an occasional drink of water or another forgotten thought, I seldom hear another word from them until morning.

"The rule is that they must go to sleep. I believe that success as a parent is in direct proportion to a parent's consistency."

Just think of the memories her children will have when they become adults. And think how the tradition can be carried on when her children become parents.

Note how exciting the parents made bedtime with the use of games and stories. The children anticipated bedtime. But also note their wisdom in helping the kids settle down with scripture stories. If the children had been sent to bed after the games, the ending would not spell success. The kids would have been so high that they couldn't settle down to sleep.

So prepare the children for bedtime. Take care of the necessary tasks first, then do something the children can anticipate.

Another vivacious young mother relates her feelings concerning the evening:

"I feel the day begins when my husband walks in the door. The boys are delighted to see their daddy and they run to him excitedly. We try to spend from 7:00 to 8:00 P.M. with our sons. We give them the opportunity to choose such activities as reading stories, listening to records, playing games, or watching a special television show. We discuss any exciting, upsetting, or memorable experiences of the day. This is such a perfect time to express our feelings for them and to share any ideas we feel are pertinent to their lives.

"After the discussions, we end the day by simply kneeling in prayer. It seems that if any words have been said in haste or if the day has been rushed, with little time to express love, it is all made right at that time."

Of course, these are suggestions for young children. But bedtime should be good for teenagers, also. With their dates and school events, it might not always be possible to spend a great deal of time with them during the evening. But if at all possible, some time should be spent with them. The length of time may be limited, but learn to make it quality time. They, too, need to have someone listen to their day's activities and their successes or failures. They need to go to bed knowing that they are loved and are in the thoughts of their parents. By all means, they should be included in the family prayer.

If your teenager is going to be out for the entire evening, place a note on top of his pillow where he'll be sure to read it. Share a thought for the day and tell him if he has something he'd like to talk about, you can easily be awakened.

Leave him a snack wrapped in plastic wrap and scribble a little poem about some humorous idea — something to make both his stomach and mind feel good before he jumps into bed.

As a teenager I never came home and found my parents asleep. Even if they were in bed, they were awake. And I knew they liked me to slip in and kiss them good night. Often I sat on the side of their bed and told them about the evening. I liked those talks. The house was quiet and it was so good to have them to myself.

I sometimes dreaded walking into the house when I knew I was late, because I knew that one of my parents would be up reading the newspaper. I much preferred the evenings when I was on time and they weren't worried and so we could talk in their bedroom. But knowing that they were *always* aware of the time, I *always* hesitated to come in late. Of course I didn't appreciate it then, but as I grow older I appreciate their concern more and more. They gave me rules to live by and they enforced them. With young children and teenagers alike, "success as a parent is in direct proportion to your consistency."

Meals! Meals! Meals!

When I was a teenager, I heard my mom say: "Meals, meals, meals! All I do is fix meals and then clean up after them. Sometimes I get so tired of having to eat!"

I shrugged off her comment, thinking she must have had a bad day and she was taking it out on her cooking. Even when I first got married, I didn't understand what Mom had really meant. Then I became a mother of three youngsters who were born within three years. Three meals a day for seven days a week started to get to me! I had to count my lucky stars, however, because Barry did relieve me of the task once a week by taking the family out to dinner or at least by picking up a pizza. But even with one night off each week, the meals still total twenty a week and over one thousand a year. That means over forty-one thousand meals in a forty-year period. That's a lot of meal planning, a lot of meal fixing, and a lot of cleaning up. I felt that either some of the eating had to stop or I had to find a better way of managing my responsibility.

Several years ago one of my good neighbors shared her meal planning schedule. She told me how she planned menus a week in advance and shopped at the store once every two weeks. This sounded feasible to me, so I went to work on a week's plan. I scheduled menus for a week and then made a list of all the groceries I needed for that time. I decided to go to the store once a week for groceries. When I made a casserole, I doubled the recipe and froze the second one. I couldn't believe the difference that planning made. Having had such success, I couldn't stop — if it felt so good to know what my menus would be for a week, how much better it would feel to have them planned for two weeks! So my next venture was scheduling menus for two weeks. This time I planned one day to do some extra baking and to make extra casseroles and meat loaves. Planning worked! I felt like a new person!

I wasn't standing in the kitchen saying to myself: "Now what will we have for dinner?" A burden had lifted from my mind. I was thinking more about exciting things to do with the kids instead of spending all that time trying to decide on a daily menu. I couldn't believe how much easier my clean-up jobs were after a meal, especially on the nights I just pulled a casserole from the freezer, made a salad, and heated a vegetable. I felt as though I had found a breakthrough which could change the plight of the everyday housewife!

Now every brain cell was alert. If a two-weeks' plan was so successful, I wondered how a monthly plan would work. So I tried it!

I gathered the family and told them my ideas. Since I felt so overwhelmed with the project, I wanted to get their opinions and food preferences. They suggested some menus which we hadn't tried for a while. I found a calendar with large daily squares and started jotting down ideas for each day.

Because I enjoy fixing a special treat for family home evening on Mondays, I planned menus which took on-the-spot preparation, such as hamburgers. For the nights when I had to be away from home for Primary or MIA or when Barry had late appointments, I selected menus which could go from freezer to oven. I tried to vary the menus so we didn't have spaghetti one night and tacos the next. Since I use the same meat filling for tacos as I use for burritos, I listed tacos once the first week and burritos once the second week.

After planning the menus, I made the grocery list by going through the scheduled recipes and writing down all the needed ingredients. The next morning I went to the store.

At first I intended to make the frozen-food dishes as well as bake the breads, cakes, and cookies in one day. But, as I quickly realized, that would be next to impossible! So I scheduled the two days following the grocery shopping day for monthly "kitchen days." The first day I did the main dishes. Imagine my feeling the first time I put fifteen pounds of hamburger, and four pounds of cheese along with several cans of sauces on the counter. I panicked! Could I really do all that cooking in one day?

I attacked the spaghetti sauces first. For containers I used the large peanut butter jars with lids. (I still use peanut butter jars for containers and have not yet had any crack. But don't pour boiling mixtures in them.) I filled them with sauce, leaving an inch head space for expansion. Looking at my first four jars of spaghetti sauce cheered me on, assuring me that I could finish the task.

Since I had often made taco filling, I started on that next. Hamburger was browned in two skillets, then I mixed the cooked meat with sauce in a large pan on the stove. My kitchen had really come to life. The children wandered in and out to see how it was going. (They seemed especially cooperative — I think they sensed how nervous I was about the whole project.) I got a little carried away with the taco filling and made enough for four taco meals and four burrito meals. But I knew that we would eventually use the filling. In fact, that put me ahead on the next month's preparation.

After finishing the taco mixture, I started browning meat for lasagna. While the noodles were cooking, the meat was browning, and the sauce was boiling, I cleaned out the freezer section of my refrigerator and put in the cooled sauces and prepared meat. (To prevent bottle breakage, don't put hot containers of food in the freezer.) After preparing three dishes of lasagna (I had extra noodles so I made an extra recipe), I *still* had some ground beef left. So I made patties, putting waxed paper or plastic wrap between them, and froze them.

I next sliced my boneless, cooked ham into the meal-size portions. Ham was scheduled for Sunday. As I cut the ham and wrapped it in aluminum foil, I thought how exciting it would be Sunday morning to take ham, bread sticks, and brownies from the freezer, to wrap some potatoes in aluminum foil for baking, to set a jello salad and to cut up a tossed salad. For dessert we would have chilled peaches with the brownies. The ham and potatoes could be baking while we were at Sunday School. Why, with less that half an hour of preparation, we could have our entire Sunday meal cooked and ready to eat. I was ecstatic! At last Sunday could become my day of rest, with time to do more spiritual things rather than spending my time in the kitchen. And the clean-up would be absolutely minimal.

Some of our meals I couldn't prepare ahead and freeze, such as the roast. But with the largest part of my meals now in the freezer, I knew the monthly planning could really work.

The first two months of this scheduling were the most difficult. I didn't know exactly how many servings to fix. But this came with experience, and I wrote notes to myself and to aid in future planning and preparing.

An example of one of my month's menus is included in this chapter. The kids wanted fish, hoagie sandwiches, and roast. Barry wanted tacos, ham, and turkey steaks.

The menus which require the most preparation and clean-up are listed on Mondays.

Since I have MIA on Wednesday, I use my taco or burrito menus because they are extra quick and require little clean-up.

Thursdays I go to the store to shop for milk and fresh produce, so I usually have ingredients for fresh salads and fresh fruits to accompany the meals throughout the week. I put the menus specifically needing fresh mushrooms, lunch meat, or other perishable foods on Thursday and Friday.

Saturday is my evening off, even though I occasionally prepare homemade pizza. Not every Saturday do we have pizza, but it's still called our "pizza night"!

On the calendar I list only the main dish, but in my head I know what the rest of the menu will be. When I first began using this method, I jotted down the entire menu.

My food storage plays a large role in my planning. With my bottled fruit, canned vegetables and an ample supply of potatoes, I can be flexible, yet prepared.

Every month when I am making my grocery list for the two

Monthly Menu Calendar

Sunday	Monday	Tuesday	Wednesday	Thursday	Friday	Saturday
	1 hamburgers and fries	2 spaghetti	3 tacos	4 chicken	5 hoagie sandwiches	6 P
7 ham	8 roast and mashed potatoes	9 hot beef sandwiches	10 burritos	11 lasagna	12 veg. soup and sandwiches	13 I
14 turkey steaks	15 hamburgers and fries	16 fish fillets	17 tacos	18 chicken	19 spaghetti	20 Z
21 ham	22 roast and mashed potatoes	23 hot beef sandwiches	24 burritos	25 lasagna	26 hoagie sandwiches	27 A
28 turkey steaks	29 hamburgers and fries	30 fish fillets	31 tacos			

Saturday letters: 6 P, 13 I, 20 Z, 27 A, and Z, S

"kitchen days," I check my food storage shelves to see what items I am getting low on. In this way my food storage stays up to date. Cases of canned goods are bought, dated, and rotated. It is a good feeling to have my month's baking done and full shelves of food!

I spend the second monthly "kitchen day" baking breads, bread sticks, cakes, cookies, and brownies. This is my children's favorite day. They are eager to help and are especially delighted when they can be my tasters. I can't bake too many loaves of bread ahead because the freezer in the top of the refrigerator is small, but I squeeze in as many baked goods as I can.

Even though the children were young and underfoot during my early baking days, they learned to anticipate that time of the month. They were invited to sit at the counter and help me crack the eggs, stir the dough, or to do other small tasks. They also seemed to like the idea that I was fixing some of the things they had suggested. In part, they realized that even though they were young, their ideas were considered and respected.

Now, after four years of incorporating monthly meal planning into my time schedule, the benefits grow as my family grows and becomes involved in extra activities and practices. Planning menus for a month is now easy. It is just as easy for me to shop for a month's needs at the grocery store as it was to shop for a week's. Now that I don't worry every day about meal planning, I can sit and listen to the children as they come home from school and look over their school papers. Consequently, we have shared some special moments.

With our meals planned and prepared ahead, the kitchen is left free for us to do some baking just for fun. The children and I love to experiment with original recipes.

Early one Saturday the kids were sitting at the counter waiting for breakfast. Saturday morning is special to them because they can have cold cereal for breakfast. That particular day they chose Rice Krispies. Barry left early for work and told us he would be home about 1:00 P.M., then we could go and do something together. Still in my nightgown, I joined the children at the table. Then it happened!

Jeff started to read the Rice Krispies box and said excitedly:

"Mom, let's enter the Rice Krispies contest. All we have to do is make up a recipe with Rice Krispies."

Cori and Scotty got excited too, especially when Jeff read what the prizes were. We didn't even take time to get dressed. We pulled things out of the cupboards and before long we were right in the middle of originating a new recipe. We must have tried about six or seven ideas. Then we struck gold! We melted caramels in margarine and then added the Rice Krispies. Next we rolled the mixture into one-inch balls. Mm-m-, delicious! To make them even more exotic, we dipped the balls into melted white chocolate. As the kids licked their fingers from dipping, they couldn't believe the yummy treat they had just invented.

"What will we name them?" asked Cori.

We were stumped. We thought of "Karmel Krunchies," "Krispy Karamels," "White Caramel Balls," and myriad other names, but we couldn't settle on one.

As I looked around the cluttered kitchen counter and at the three excited children sitting there, the idea struck me.

"What's the sweetest thing we know that is topped in white?" I asked the kids. They looked all around, but couldn't guess.

"Okay," I said. "*Who's* the sweetest thing we know topped in white?"

Jeff and Cori looked at Scotty with his pretty white hair and chimed together, "Scotty!"

"Let's call them 'Scotties,'" I suggested, and they all agreed that the name was perfect.

I got the camera as the children ran to get dressed so they wouldn't be in their pajamas for pictures. I photographed them tasting the "Scotties."

Just as I was snapping the last picture, Barry walked in. There I stood, still in my nightgown and the kitchen a mess! But he knew that we must have had an exciting morning because the kids were bubbling about the contest. As soon as the prints were developed, we submitted our entry complete with pictures and the story of how "Scotties" were named.

We didn't win the contest, but that recipe is a real winner in our family. Many times we have made "Scotties" for treats for our neighbors or for special occasions. Not only have the neighbors delighted in the treat, but they have asked for the recipe. Many times Scotty has mentioned that probably no other boy has a recipe named after him. He sometimes accompanies me to the neighbors just to see if they like the "Scotties." When they get excited about the treats, it seems to tell Scotty that they really like *him* too. In fact, so much good has developed from that Saturday morning that now Jeff and Cori have recipes named after them too. We became so excited about creating new recipes that we even compiled a book *Kids in the Kitchen* with illustrations of Jeff, Cori and Scott on the cover.

Many times our kitchen has been the center of stimulating projects which have brought us closer together as a family, such as the annual Easter egg coloring event. Barry takes over. As I boil the eggs and set them on the counter to dry, he is getting the dye and paints ready. He gets all of the children into action. We paint in every way imaginable and Barry takes great pride in painting the most unusual design each year. For an entire afternoon our kitchen is full of giggles and ohs and ahs as the white eggs become creative works of art.

If my mind were still cluttered with worries of what we were "having for dinner," I doubt that I would be so eager to make my working place a playing place. Thanks to my monthly meal planning, we have made memories worth remembering for eternity!

Write Me a Letter

When our first child was born, I can remember thinking that I would never forget the joy of hearing the first cry of our baby or the way I felt when I saw Barry holding him in the delivery room. But part of that feeling does escape parents and that is why it is important to record special feelings at the time they occur.

After each new child was born, I wrote a page in his baby book. I shared with him the feelings in my heart and soul. I let him know how much he was wanted by his mom and dad and how lucky we felt to get him. The pages are emotional and sentimental, but so were the occasions. Those pages are the first pages of each child's life story.

In order to keep their life stories up to date, I devised a very simple plan, using a calendar. Every three months I put at the top of the page, "write a letter to kids." This is my reminder so that I don't neglect writing. Throughout the three months I jot on the calendar little incidents which happen. (If the idea is quite detailed, I write more information on a separate slip of paper and clip it to the calendar.) I select a day during the third month and type a letter to each child recalling the moments we've shared, the things he's accomplished, and the feelings of Barry and myself. Since all of the reminders and dates are on the calendar, it takes me only ten or fifteen minutes to write a page. What treasures we can create in such short periods of time!

The days I write their letters are most special. I usually read each child's letter to him and ask if there is something I've forgotten to mention. They love to recall exciting moments.

At the end of every letter I close with a special message from Barry and me. It is a perfect time to express our feelings concerning them. The letter is dated and signed by both parents and put into a manila envelope. Each child has an envelope which contains all of his letters. When each child gets married, his letters will be bound and given to him as a wedding gift. Of course, as the children grow older, they will be encouraged to keep their own personal journals even though I shall continue writing letters.

The sample letter that follows was written to our daughter:

"Dearest Cori,

"It has been nearly a week now since your nursery school teacher, Mrs. Smith, called me to say that you are such a special little girl. She didn't have to tell me that because Dad, Jeff, Scotty and I already know that. But she wanted the chance to tell of your vast development in school also. She proceeded to tell me that you are very kind to the children and that you have been befriending some of the little quiet and shy children who really need a friend. She commented on your ability to be a leader and how you can get things organized or can direct the children into different types of activities.

"During the past four months, I have seen this come out in you also. You have been very kind to little Scotty and have included him in much of your activity. You have much energy and such an ability to find humor and laugh at it. Many times Dad will tell a rather dry joke and you will pick it out and just roar until you have all of us laughing.

"You are enjoying your creative dancing. You like being good in what you do. Forever I will recall with fondness the day you and I went to buy your dancing shoes. We went to the top of a building in Bountiful to a little shop called the Prima Donna. A kind lady tried some slippers on you. Then she tried a cute lime green dance suit on you. (We had only enough money for the shoes, so we had to leave the suit.) We bought your ballet shoes and the minute you got home, you put them on. You kept telling me how much you loved them as you danced about the house. When Daddy came home, you sidled up to him and gently gave him a kiss, whispering, 'Thanks for my dancing shoes.'

"That night when I went in to tuck the covers around you, in your arms was the pink box with your dancing shoes inside.

"Daddy and I hope and pray for you each day that you'll always keep this sweetness about you and that you will always have reason to be happy and vibrant.

"We sure do love you."

Another type of record the children are keeping is a scrap-book in which they put selected school papers, birthday cards, and little mementos they want to keep.

When the children started school, I was amazed at the number of papers they brought home each day. They felt that each one of their papers was very important and so I felt guilty about throwing them away, but we couldn't save them all unless we added on to our home! We tried a new plan. All of their papers went on the kitchen door where we could all admire their work. Then, at the end of the week, we looked over the papers and picked out those which really stood out as "important." Those papers I put away on a shelf. When the time came to work on scrapbooks, we again sorted through their papers and decided which were most important. Those selected were put into the scrapbooks.

Once every six months we designate a day to get our scrap-books up to date. At that time, we also take out their picture albums, one for each of them. They can then choose from our latest prints one or two recent photos which are meaningful to them to add to their albums. In this way, when they are old enough to leave home, each will have his own photo album without having to go to the family album and to take our prints.

Our children are young enough that I am still keeping baby books for them. That will probably come to an end as each starts his own book of remembrance. Meaningful pictures go into their baby books along with notes of things they say or do and informa-tion as to their health.

At first it might sound like a lot of work to keep all of these

books for all of your children. But think about it again and you will
see how simple it is.

1. Once every three months write a letter to each child and
   add to his manila envelope.
2. Once every six months take the scrapbooks off the shelf
   and bring them up to date.
3. When the kids are working on their scrapbooks, take out
   the baby books and bring them up to date.
4. Once every six months take out the most recent photos
   and let each child pick only one or two for his individual
   album. That's only a few pictures per year, but the way
   time flies those pictures will add up very soon in an album.

These are only suggestions. Do the type of books which fit
your life-style.

A mother whose children are old enough to write has the
family gather on Sunday afternoon and they all write in their
journals the happenings of the week. Not only will her children
have priceless records, but the mother and father will also be
keeping their own records. The more we can do things like this as
a family, the more meaning the experiences hold.

One mother with four young boys has said that she likes to
write them each one long letter at the end of the year. Just think
how valuable those nineteen or twenty letters will be to her boys
when they set out to meet the world. Don't procrastinate, it's
difficult to backtrack. There's no substitute for current recordings.
If your life suddenly ended, think how invaluable those letters
would be to those who love you.

Once after I gave a lecture on keeping a "Book of Living," a
grandmother came to me and asked if she could have a copy of
some of my material.

"I have two special granddaughters," she said. "Their mother
(my daughter) died and they are left with no records of her
feelings, even though their lives together were close and meaningful. They played together, dreamed together, and had a beautiful
relationship. But my granddaughters need to have in writing what
their mother was like and how she felt about each of her little girls.
Although the words won't be the same ones my daughter would

have used, I am going to write my daughter's story and give it to my little granddaughters on their birthdays. I am also going to give them a journal to start writing in so that their little girls will have that record which I wish my granddaughters now had."

This good grandmother didn't stop with just her two little granddaughters. She bought journals for her sons, her husband, her other grandchildren, and for herself. She has seen to it that everyone dear to her has a journal for keeping some kind of record.

When one mother heard my lecture on ways to keep children's records, she said, "I wish I had known that twenty-five years ago. Most of my children are now married and have their own little children."

But she realized it wasn't too late to begin. She started writing the life story of each of her six children, as she and her husband remembered them. "This project will probably take me a whole year to do," she said. "But this Christmas they will each be given their story as recalled by Mom and Dad." What a gift! Could there be any better?

One devoted grandmother I know has a flair for writing poetry. For her grandchildren's birthdays, she recaptures the moments shared with them during the year in a poem.

So write a letter, a story, a poem, or even a note to your children. Let them see in black and white the growth they are making in their lives. Let them partake of the knowledge you and your mate have gained while being their parents. Let them know of the hopes and dreams you have for them. It is a perfect way to say:

> "We love you,
> Mom and Dad."

Sense Your Children's Feelings

Sometimes the routine of daily life makes it possible to get into ruts. Some mothers feel that they need to get away from the same environment they've had day after day. Many times they leave the children with a baby-sitter and then go to lunch with the girls. This may be fine occasionally, but let me share a discovery.

When we four were all in the house together and Barry was at work, sometimes the constant home environment bothered the children also. One particular day I got a baby-sitter, but instead of leaving all the children home while I left, I invited one to go on a date with me. Thereafter each would have a turn at going to lunch and on a date. The children decided Jeff could go first because he was the oldest.

We left behind the worries of home and the everyday tasks. We chose a place he wanted to go for lunch. Then he chose to go to the 7-Eleven store so he could look at the toys and have an Icee. We had lots of fun! We talked about *him*. We rambled about his favorite games, his fantasies, and whatever came into his mind. I got to know my son better that day. He brought me into his world, and he taught me a valuable lesson.

In order to get to *know* our children, we have to let them talk their "lingo" and we need to listen to every word. They don't view life quite the same as adults, and it is refreshing to be lifted out of our world for a while and to listen to the dreams of a youngster.

The "Mommy dates" became anticipated events. But when Barry decided it was time for some "Daddy dates," the excitement really grew. Barry purchased season tickets for some college football games. He invited one of the children to go with him on a date. The two who had to wait their turns talked about the upcoming date for days and weeks.

Barry recalls his date with Scotty:

"Although Scott was only three years old and too young to understand much about football, we had a great day together. He talked constantly about everything. He enjoyed the popcorn, hot dogs, and pop. But most of all, he liked the two of us being together, with me giving him undivided attention.

"About the third quarter of the game, he laid his head on my knee and went to sleep. I couldn't stand and see the exciting plays. The actual game and score has already been forgotten, but for father and son the day will be a lasting memory."

One of the special daddy dates occurs when Barry takes a child with him on the motorcycle into the hills near our home. As they travel the dirt roads together, they share memorable experiences.

Once Barry took Cori for an extra long ride. At the crest of the mountain Barry decided to turn off the motorcycle to let it cool for a while. He coasted downhill with Cori hugging him tightly from the back. They heard the birds chirping in the trees and the leaves and twigs crackling under the wheels of the bike. Suddenly they were startled by the sound of rattles. Barry stopped the bike immediately before running over a large rattlesnake which was sunning itself in the middle of the dirt path.

What an exciting story they had to tell us as they arrived home! In fact, Cori's brothers wanted to hear the story over and over, and we could sense that they hoped someday they could find a rattlesnake when they went with their dad.

I recall an evening I shared with all three children. A new restaurant was opening in town and Roger Staubach, quarterback for the Dallas Cowboys football team, was to be there signing autographs. Our children think Dallas has the greatest football team in the country, so the quarterback is naturally a hero for them. Since Barry was out of town on business, I was elected to pick them up immediately after Primary and to take them to see Roger Staubach. For three days every conversation at mealtime had been about this forthcoming momentous afternoon. Because of their electric vibrations, even I became excited!

The great day finally arrived — and with it heavy rain. As I pulled up to the curb all three children came running out of the building, their faces beaming with excitement. I envisioned a hurried trip into the city which would require only an hour out in the terrible downpour; but when we arrived at the restaurant, the rain was pouring even harder. There was a line of Dallas fans circling the building.

"Don't worry," said Jeff. "That line should move pretty fast."

The kids wore their Dallas football shirts and wouldn't put on their coats because they wanted their idol to see their shirts. But after standing in rain and wind for fifteen minutes and having moved forward only three feet, they decided to get their coats.

We stood in the rain for another hour and fifteen minutes before finally squeezing inside the building. The kids shed their coats, and I could feel their anticipation as they spotted their hero. They finally got his autograph and then we bought some take-out chicken to celebrate the occasion.

I didn't realize how important that evening was to the children until we got back in the car and Jeff turned to me and said: "Gosh, Mom, I think this is the greatest thing that has ever happened in my life. I'll never forget this night!" Cori and Scotty chimed their agreement.

Tears were running down my cheeks as fast as the rain had been running down my back, and I was grateful that I hadn't doused their enthusiasm.

Being aware of children's needs should be a constant concern for parents. I am convinced that if we pray diligently for guidance in raising our children, we will somehow know when we must come to their aid. This has been proven to me many times in just the few short years I have been a parent. One incident was so close to being tragic that I shudder to think what could have happened had Barry and I not had some help from the Lord.

Being sandwiched between boys who are a year older and two years younger makes it difficult for a little girl to find her real identity. Whenever Cori wanted to play with her dolls, her brothers automatically gave her a cap gun and a cowboy hat and invited her to play with them. Because she could run as fast and play as hard as they did, she was very comfortable for a couple of years. But then I started to notice some pattern breaks. She hit her little brother and often seemed to take satisfaction in seeing him cry. She created trouble and showed off to get my attention. And she would say things to hurt my feelings. I began to sense that she was not happy. At the time, Cori was enrolled in a preschool kindergarten and she was also having difficulty there.

My adult friends said that she was just "going through a stage" — she'd be fine. But my spirit would not rest. I lay awake nights worrying about her and wondering what her father and I could do to help her. I can remember waking Barry at three in the morning to tell him of my worries and concerns. He said that he would make a special effort to single Cori out and to show her more attention. Also, he would make sure that he gave her lots of hugs and kisses and let her know that he thought she was the neatest girl in the world. In our prayers we asked for help in knowing what to do.

One morning I stood looking out the window; I seemed to be searching for an answer. How could I help her find internal happiness? The wisdom came when I needed it most. That evening I talked to Barry about my idea, and he agreed that it was good. I called her preschool teacher and said that I felt very strongly that Cori needed to stay at home with me. For some reason Cori was very insecure as to her self-image, so I was going to make her my number one project.

The project started. I made sure each day that Cori and I found some time to be together. Whether it was to fix her hair or paint her fingernails, we did it together. We talked and talked. We discovered together her outstanding traits. She amazed me with her energy and zest for life. I had always thought her to be insensitive, but she was just the opposite. When Barry went to the store or for a short ride, he took her along. We didn't buy her presents, but we poured our love and attention upon her. Of course, we had to be careful to make sure the boys didn't feel slighted.

When Cori and I went to the drive-in for lunch, we always ordered one malt with two straws. She loved the idea of sharing. I made it a habit to always take hold of her hand and squeeze it. I told her repeatedly how much I loved her. She had been a premature baby with hyaline membrane disease. We nearly lost her. So I told her often of the frightening experience at the hospital. Her eyes twinkled when I told her how we finally got to take her home from the hospital and how all the neighbors came to look at her through the window. I told her how Jeff brought all of his toys to her. He couldn't believe he had a baby sister. She heard the story so many times that I thought she would tire of it, but the story was just another way of letting her know how vital and important she was to her family.

After about six months of constant effort and with Cori sometimes showing some regression, Barry and I began to see her change. She didn't hit her little brother as often and she started to settle down in her Sunday School class. Every Sunday she told us how hard she tried to sit still and she was so proud when she knew she had done it. I'll never forget one Primary day when she looked at me before going into the building and said, "Mom, I'm going to try so hard today to sit still." Then she kissed me and ran into the building.

After the meeting as I drove the car into the parking lot to pick up the children, I saw Cori. She had a broad grin and her brown eyes twinkled. She slid down the railing about three times and then turned and ran to the car. "Guess what, Mom!" she blurted. "I sat still the whole time of Primary!" She had won her battle. She was no longer the bad little girl of her class. She felt the joy of being good and she wanted more of that feeling.

Cori knows she is very important. She knows she is loved and she knows she is a good person. Her self-image is shining. She is sensitive to and aware of the feelings of others. I shudder to think how the picture could be, had I not stood by the window one day years ago and prayed for the knowledge of what to do. As parents, we have so much help waiting if we are but wise enough to seek it. By working together, with the help of the Lord, a mother and father can perform miracles.

Cori's experiences have been recorded in her journal. I hope that her story will be a source of strength to her when she is a parent raising her own little sons and daughters.

Take the time to sense the inner feelings of your children. Pray for constant guidance and help in doing what is best for them. If there is a problem, act upon solving it. Some stages of growing up have obstacles in the pathway which might discourage the child and make him turn the other way. We must be aware of these obstacles!

Add the Zest of Anticipation

Introduce your child to the appetizer of life's menu: anticipation. Anticipating his birthday, his first day of school, his first real horseback ride, his first airplane trip, his first meeting at Cub Scouts can add zest to a child's desire for living. You are teaching him to be aware of approaching days and events, and he knows that when one day ends, there will be another. This is especially good for a child to know when one day has been disappointing for him. He will not give up in despair thinking all is lost, because he knows there are other things waiting for him.

Let me share a positive episode with our family. Soon after our youngest arrived, the other two said they wanted to go to Disneyland. Most of their friends had been there and they felt left out. Barry and I discussed the idea, but we had reservations. First, the baby would have to be carried everywhere we went. Second, the children were so young that they might not remember the trip in years to come. We sat down and talked with the children about the problems and then we made a deal. When baby Scotty was four years old, we would go to Disneyland. That way, all three could enjoy and remember the trip. "But what if we have another baby then?" wailed our daughter.

"If so, we will still go and work out those little problems," Dad assured them.

Four years to a child, and sometimes to an adult, can seem like an eternity. But we started putting pennies and other coins into a poodle bank and said that that would be our spending money. Instead of putting pennies into gum machines, they were encouraged to add to the trip funds (thereby giving us a reason to leave the gum machines alone).

I know it sounds unbelievable, but we waited until the summer Scotty turned four and then went to Disneyland. We had talked about it for all that time and had kept the trip alive in the minds of the children. They were impatient and wanted to go immediately. But when the time actually came to go on our trip, the entire family was excited. And I might add that we had a grand time.

Barry and I once went to Hawaii for a vacation and when we came back, we told the children of this beautiful place that we wanted to take them. So already we are talking about the summer we all go to Hawaii when they are teenagers.

Anticipating events as a family not only provides the time to save financially for the event; it also gives an opportunity for the entire group to be working toward a common goal.

One of the highlights of each year is the ward father and son outing. The event is anticipated months in advance. Barry, Jeff, and Scott spend overnight at a campsite and hike and play games. Usually they see a movie outdoors the first evening.

The first year Barry and Jeff found a large hawk feather. Jeff had started kindergarten and he was excited to take his feather for "show and tell." He still has his feather and it reminds him of the outing with his father.

When the boys head for the outing, Cori and I plan our special time together. We do some shopping and go out for dinner, but the thing she seems to like the most is crawling into bed with me and having the chance to talk and talk about anything she wants and for as long as she wants.

Anticipation does not have to cover a long period of time. Anticipate the first snowfall. Anticipate evening and the chance to play a game together. Occasionally, however, we have anticipated a grand evening and then all of the kids are in a rotten mood or a telephone call takes my husband away for the evening and everything goes sour. Inevitably those times will occur; but it doesn't mean we can't be excited about the next day.

Anticipate and plan for the holidays. You don't necessarily have to go all out and spend a lot of money. But a cherry pie and a birthday song on George Washington's birthday take only a few minutes. On that day let the kids tell you what they know about the father of our country.

I'll never forget one Fourth of July in particular. It was the bicentennial year, 1976. I had directed part of a play concerning the bicentennial and my children had been in the cast. So I felt we had done our part in recognizing the great event. But that Sunday morning, July Fourth, I felt a great need to acknowledge that *one* day and not have it part of the whole year's celebration. So we all went to our closets and picked out clothes that had the colors red, white, and blue in them. (Poor Scotty — the only white pants he had were too short, but we laughed about it and he wore them anyway.) I made cupcakes and cookies all decorated in red, white, and blue frosting. We then got out some large flags and also some red, white, and blue streamers and decorated the outside of our house. We even had balloons hanging from the railing of our porch. In the middle of these decorations, we added a gigantic sign reading, "Happy Birthday America!" That was a special day for us and we surely had lots of fun celebrating. I know some of the neighbors must have wondered why we would go to all of that effort, but the kids will always remember the bicentennial Fourth of July.

Anticipate each child's birthday with him. Again, I do not advocate going to the store and spending a lot of money. One of the best birthday parties we have had was for Jeff. He wanted to do something very different and we spent days trying to decide what it could be. Then one afternoon we were driving in the car and he noticed the huge white letter *B* on the mountain. "I want to take a hike on my birthday and climb to the letter *B*," he said.

The afternoon of his birthday found Cori, Scotty, a favorite friend, the "birthday kid," and me on the mountainside with our sticks and jugs of water. It was in the fall and the mountain was dry and dusty. The kids delighted in kicking up as much dust as they could. We found a dead snake which they carried on the end of a stick. We disturbed several lizards who were lazily basking in the hot sun. And, of course, there were the grasshoppers and bees who joined our hike. We talked about what we would do if a rattlesnake crawled by or what would happen if one of us fell and broke a leg. Sometimes we were practical and sometimes we joked. The pictures I took of the birthday party weren't the typical party-type photos. They were pictures of very dusty, dirty little children who had big grins on their faces, thinking they were every bit as brave and strong as Lewis and Clark.

Each time we plan a party, I try to discourage the kids from including events which cost a lot of money. Barry and I want them to know how to have good, exciting times with little expense. We hope this will teach them that they usually can make their own happiness if they try.

Improve Your Communcation

I f parents desire to truly communicate with their children, they must be willing to use not only their voices, but their eyes, ears, and hearts as well.

A father relates the following experience in communicating with his nine-year-old son:

"My son and I didn't seem to be able to talk with each other. Every time I decided it was time for us to discuss a problem or whatever, he just clammed up. Then I got an idea to start interviewing him. Maybe through the interviews we would be able to start communicating, I thought. So I told him about my idea and we scheduled the following Sunday for the first 'father and son' interview.

"Sunday arrived and my son and I sat down together. I asked him some basic questions and then expressed some of my desires concerning his life. Each week the interviews were about the same. But one particular week, he told me about some of his feelings. He even told me about something he had done wrong. I was uneasy. In fact, I got a little upset.

" 'You see, Dad,' said my boy, 'that's why I can't talk with you. You always get so mad.'

"I realized that I hadn't been trying to talk *with* my son. I had been talking *to* him. I had placed him on a pedestal and hadn't allowed him room to make mistakes. I thought of my growing-up years and admitted many mistakes I had made. From most of them I had learned valuable lessons.

"After my self-evaluation, I again talked with my son. I told him I wasn't being fair. I expressed my feelings about being his parent, but still being in the situation of learning. I owned up to mistakes I had made as a father and asked him if he'd like to try our interviews once more, only this time it would be a true father and son interview.

"First I interviewed him and it was my responsibility to really listen. Not only was I concerned about *what* he did but I also considered the *whys* and *hows*. Then my son interviewed me. It was a perfect time to express some of the frustrations I felt as a parent. I found my son's comments and suggestions very helpful. We spent nearly two hours together in that interview. We really communicated!"

Sometimes our children can give simple solutions for our seemingly burdensome frustrations. For example, one afternoon I was particularly uptight with the children. My little girl had spilled the glue all over the table and I felt my nerves becoming like hot wires. I started to raise my voice and gradually it turned into a yell. I was standing on the stairs with the two youngest sitting on the floor looking up at me, and the oldest standing about an arm's length away. Just before I turned to go upstairs my four-year-old son said in a low voice: "Mom, you don't need to yell at us. Why don't you just talk to us?" His little sister who had spilled the glue started to cry. "Cori just needs to know you love her," he said.

I felt the tears sting my eyes. I knew he was right. I gathered them to me and I hugged my little daughter. We sat on the floor, and with them in front of me I looked into their honest, young eyes and apologized for the way I had acted. I told them that I was tired, the baby had kept me up during the night and I needed some more sleep. But I told them that I would try not to yell at them anymore. There were eager and quick to forgive.

I had always known that it wasn't good to yell at children, but hearing the feelings of my children made me resolve not to raise my voice. Sometimes I still find myself ready to break loose and raise the roof, but I'll never forget that afternoon. I can still see the expression on my son's face and the wisdom in his blue eyes when he asked me to just "talk" to them.

From what I observe, it isn't just the Erickson children who don't like to be yelled at. When our oldest started third grade, he and his friends were discussing their new teacher. "She's so great! She never yells," commented the little friend. Overhearing his statement reinforced my belief that yelling is not the way to communicate with children.

But how do we get across our ideas and discipline without raising our voices to get their attention? A wise father decided he would try a unique idea. He initiated citations — citations for good behavior and citations for bad behavior. During the week family members issued citations to other members. Then on family night members of the family took turns reading the citations they had received. The citations for good behavior were read first. It was an excellent time for parents and brothers and sisters to add their positive ideas and praise for one another. If parents have foresight, citations for good behavior will be more abundant than those for bad behavior. This approach can get the family into the habit of looking for the good in those with whom they live.

When the family members read their citations for bad behavior, such as not keeping a straight room, the rest of the family members become the judge. They can declare one of three decisions: 1. They can totally forgive; 2. They can give a light penalty; 3. They can issue a stiff penalty (but this must be done with much wisdom). By using the citation approach, parents can achieve several objectives.

1. Each family member will look for the good in others.
2. Children will observe more closely some of the tasks (which many times are taken for granted) performed by their parents. This will help the children appreciate the value of their parents.
3. The "good" citations are another form of praise, which encourage the children to keep up their good work. Much good accomplished by children often goes unobserved, such as a happy laugh or an eagerness to please the parent.

4. By knowing a "bad" citation might be given, it is hoped that the children (and parents) will try harder to do what they know will earn a citation for good behavior.
5. Family members will have the chance to judge and a chance to be judged. Therefore, they will have an opportunity to learn fairness and justice.
6. Having the option to fully forgive can teach each member to be compassionate and forgiving.

Of course, the citations and rules must be adjusted to fit each family. But if parents keep the correct perspectives in mind, a project such as this one can be valuable.

Another way we communicate with our children is by playing with them. One father admitted that his son is a poor loser. In talking to the boy about the problem the father said that he, too, liked to win. He suggested to his son that when they played a physical sport where the father had the advantage, the son could choose one of two rules. Number one, the father would play his hardest and best and he probably would win. Number two, the father would play his second best and give the son the better odds. His son liked the idea. Sometimes the son chose the first rule because he wanted the full challenge; other times he chose the second rule. "Even when he knows that I am playing my second best, he gets satisfaction out of winning. I feel that honesty is the best policy in dealing with our children. I could have faked that I was playing my best and let him beat me, but he would have been able to sense my dishonesty. Not only do we have great fun together in sports and games, but he knows that he can trust me," said the father.

Another way of communicating with our children is by working together. Let them help with the household chores. It is their home also; and if they work in it, they will have more feeling of belonging.

I was raised in a rural area and when my brothers were working in the fields, I was working in the home. We never asked our brothers or father to do much in the home because we felt they did their work outdoors. But life in the city is different.

Our sons have their duties to do in the home. It takes nothing from their masculinity to have them dump the garbage or vacuum the carpet. It would be unfair to them to let them think that a home is kept clean by magic. If a home is to sparkle and if nutritious meals are to be served each day, a great deal of work is involved. Divide the work up and it becomes fun and easy.

Make your children feel like they are really needed to keep the home going. When we get ready to clean the house, the kids all pitch in with such jobs as vacuuming, dusting, and straightening. Once my little boy said: "Gosh, Mom, we do all of your work. Aren't you glad you don't have to do any?" I chuckled and agreed. He felt so important, just as though everything would fall through if it weren't for him.

When you are just starting to get help from the children, list the jobs to be done and let the children choose the task they want to do. Then alternate the jobs each week.

As a mother, use their help to your advantage. I like to have time to write, so I initiate their help before they go to school. Before they leave they vacuum the floor, straighten their rooms, make their beds, and wash the dishes. With a clean house and previously prepared meals, I am free to get to those things of my choice.

After we had purchased a lot which had to have many trees cut down, we gathered the children, had them put on their old work clothes, and then gave them each a pair of gloves. Each child had been saving for an anticipated purchase, but they had not found enough ways to earn money. So Barry told them that if they worked hard and stuck to the job, they could earn some money to use toward that pogo stick, hat, or watch.

They worked like hired hands, gathering the logs, stacking the wood, and piling the brush. Barry told them how strong they would become if they worked like that all the time. When we were right in the middle of our day's work, I happened to glance at our son. He was struggling to lift a log. Finally he got it in his arms and lugged it over to the woodpile. Then he pulled up his shirt sleeve and examined his muscle to see if it had grown. He was excited to have been given the chance to earn money, to build his muscles, and to help his parents.

Make the working experience meaningful and let the children know you appreciate their efforts. If you can afford it, give them a chance to earn some spending money, but if you can't afford it, don't make money an issue. We have many more days ahead of us which will be spent working on the lot, but the children will not earn money each time.

The main reward for working is the one later expressed by our son who was flexing his muscle while working. That night he got me all alone and said: "That sure was fun working in the trees today. Every time I tried to lift a big log which was heavy, I thought to myself how proud Dad would be of me if I could lift those big logs. Every time I thought of Dad, it seemed that I could lift the log." Now that is a great reward!

Earning good grades in school is another kind of work. The way in which we work with our children as they are solving math problems or learning to spell communicates many things to them.

Communicate praise when your child brings a nice-looking paper home. Barry's mother is a schoolteacher of third graders. She says that it breaks her heart when some of her little students finish a paper and then throw it into the garbage. She tells them to take their papers home for their parents to see. They often answer: "Why bother? They never look at my papers anyway."

Thank heaven for good teachers who communicate praise for work well done. At the first of the year our little girl was hurrying through her assignments and was not doing very neat work. When her teacher started to write "pretty work" on those papers which were done well, her work really improved.

Another way of communicating with our children is by direct eye contact. A father of a little retarded daughter said that she taught him true communication.

"She cannot speak any words, even though she is six years old," he relates. "But when I look directly into her eyes, she seems to understand my ideas and especially my different moods. She can sense if I am truly glad to be with her and she can sense if I am in a hurry and don't have the time for her. Since our means of communicating are very limited, I have to take the time to look into her eyes as I speak to her."

Direct eye contact doesn't work only with retarded children. I recall taking a class in college which was to prepare me for teaching high school students. We were instructed to use direct eye contact or else we would probably lose the interest of class members. When I started teaching, I knew the value of what I had been taught. Being able to look my students right in the eye, instead of burying my head in a book while talking to them made a world of difference. I think the fact that there were few discipline problems was a result of the direct eye contact.

I recall one afternoon at home when the children and I were sitting on one of their beds reading stories. My two-year-old wanted to tell me something. I talked to him, but I wasn't looking at him. With his chubby, soft little hands on my chin, he turned my head so I could look him straight in the eye. I knew then that I had to listen with my eyes as well as with my ears.

Listening with the eyes is not confined to the young. Teen-agers thrive on your listening with your eyes and ears when they confide in you. Through direct eye contact, you can sometimes learn much more than what is being spoken. You can sense if your teenager is hurt or embarrassed or feeling guilty, just by the way he looks at you. If the relationship isn't very strong between parent and teenager, looking each other in the eye can be difficult and strained. But for a beginning try two simple phrases: "Is there anything you'd like to tell me? I would really like to listen."

Again, praise the teenager for his worthwhile efforts. Young children, parents, and teenagers thrive on praise. But praise does not mean paying a dollar for each "A" on the report card. By offering that reward you are putting a price tag on his ability to do well. If you let him experience the joy of doing his best, he knows that that feeling has no price.

Dr. Elliott Landau expressed this idea beautifully in his article "The Poor Little Rich Child."

"Children must not be bought. I know a couple who makes the payoff every report card time. An 'A' equals one dollar. Too often these same people resort to the trickery of money to persuade their children to be righteous.

"I can never forget the gentleman who came to me with the tale of how he, in order to teach his children how much $5,000 was, arranged for a dinner in a local restaurant and placed 5,000 one-dollar bills in a pile before his family.

"At the proper moment in the evening he dramatically swept the cover from the mound of bills exposing the treasure and then told his family that for each of them there was this initial payment if they would only promise to tread the straight and narrow." (*Deseret News,* May 2, 1978. Used with permission.)

Sometimes our actions communicate wrong ideas; we need to examine the total effect of our actions *before* we act.

Another means of communicating with our family is by praying together. In our home we have noticed that even if there have been arguments and hurt feelings during the day, when we gather together as a family and one of the members says the prayer, many problems are resolved as he prays for everyone, even the offender.

I'll never forget a time when our children were just getting old enough to say the blessing on the food. My parents came to visit us and as we gathered for our meal, one of the children wanted to say the blessing. Throughout his prayer he not only blessed the food, but he also kept thanking Heavenly Father for his grandpa and grandma and that they could come and eat with us. I could sense the joy which my parents felt in knowing that they were so welcome.

When we have our family prayer and it is either Barry's or my turn to pray, not only do we communicate love to our children as we thank the Father for them, but we also pray for our relatives, friends, and neighbors.

One of our sons had a real problem in getting along with one of the neighbor boys. Sometimes it was very difficult for him to say anything good about the boy. Both boys irritated each other. So they went their separate ways. One day we heard that the neighbor boy was critically ill. In fact, his parents didn't know if he would live. We told the children about the boy's condition — then we turned the situation around. I asked the boys: "What would you feel like inside if your little sister was sick and we knew she might not be able to stay with us on earth? Even if we knew that Heavenly Father wanted her back with him, we would still miss her very much."

All of a sudden they understood how serious the situation was. We talked about it for a while longer and then knelt in a circle and said a prayer, asking Heavenly Father to help our friend get better if it was what he thought was right. I couldn't hold back the tears when my boy who had disliked the neighbor turned to me and asked if we had a present or something he could give to the boy. It had always seemed easy for our son to pray for those he loved, but at last he had experienced the joy which comes from praying for someone he didn't especially care for as a friend.

The most important lesson we teach our children by communicating with our family through prayer is to call upon their Heavenly Father when they need help. Our children hear and watch us ask the Father for guidance and direction, and we hope that they will incorporate this into their lives.

We also communicate through the tone of voice we use. To illustrate this point I'll tell of a mistake I once made. First of all, I had a dozen things on my mind — I was supposed to teach a Primary class, bake brownies for a fireside, prepare a workshop on food preparation, and call the TV repair man. My five-year-old came to me with a disgusted look on his face. "Where's my number shirt?" he asked. "I want to wear it today."

His problem seemed insignificant to me; I slightly raised my voice and said in a most disgusting tone: "I don't know where it is. If you'd put your clothes where they belong, you'd know where to find them!"

I could have said those exact words in a loving and caring tone of voice with a concerned expression on my face, and he wouldn't have walked away hurt. He had come to me for some help and even though he hadn't used the best approach either, I didn't need to add fuel to his fire and demean his self-image. Many children would have yelled back some innuendo to defend a shattered ego, but Scotty has never been a child to talk back. Luckily, I had enough sense to go into his room. He was quietly going through his clothes, trying to find his shirt.

"I'm sorry, Scotty," I said, as I joined in the search. "This morning my mind was boggled with worries, but I know that's no excuse for talking to you like that."

"Well, you just hate me," he said, as his lip quivered.

Not only had I communicated that I didn't think he was very bright for losing his shirt, but to him I had also communicated that I hated him. Too many times our children misinterpret our words when we use a harsh tone of voice.

Even when children become teenagers, they still question their self-worth when addressed in a rough and disgusted tone of voice.

A mother of an eighteen-year-old said: "When my daughter comes in at night, if I say in a voice of disgust, 'Be sure to turn off the lights,' my daughter becomes really defensive. But the tension doesn't materialize if I greet her with 'Did you have a good time? Remember the porch light. Okay?' "

I could tell when teaching English and American Literature that if I used a light tone of voice and a sprinkling of enthusiasm, the students were eager to learn the lessons. I had to be careful to control my temper so that I could stay in command of the classroom. Believe it or not, I think my control of temper and tongue made my teaching career grow into the good memories that I have now.

If I worked as hard to teach my own children as I did to teach my high school students, I would *have* to succeed as a mother. And that is the point I ponder often. The children within my home are those with whom I want to spend eternity. Are they not worth the time and effort that I would expend for children outside my home?

We communicate to our children when we discourage or encourage them in the arts and crafts. If you have a talent, share it with your child. This communicates important messages. For example, if you are good at music, share this interest with your children. If possible, include them in your creative ideas. Write a song for them and sing it to them often. Write a song they can sing with you. Encourage them to help you write the lyrics for a song and let them know you like their ideas. Let them think freely; don't discourage their comments — you will be amazed with their abilities.

I love to write my own songs. Many nights when the children are lying in bed (waiting to fall asleep) and when Barry is at a meeting, I sit in my bedroom and sing songs about the children. I use my guitar for accompaniment. Often I will hear a faint little sleepy voice say, "Please sing that song again, Mom."

Sometimes when I am stumped in the middle of writing lyrics, I ask the children for help. They have come up with some fantastic ideas which were easily incorporated into the songs. They are gradually realizing that they also have talents. Our little seven-year-old daughter jumped out of the tub one evening and with a towel wrapped around her said: "Grab your guitar, Mom. I've made up a song." Of course she has had no training in writing lyrics, but she had made up a beautiful song about her father. We hurried and found a tune to go with the words. Then after dinner she sang her song to her father. Barry was sincerely touched and Cori felt proud that she had done something so special for him.

Sharing your talents is advice to fathers also. If the father has a knack for playing football, basketball, or any sport, he can do a world of good for his children if he will work with them. Barry is great at sports. I was so excited when he took the children and me skiing and worked to teach us how to ski. He is determined that skiing will be a family sport which we can share together through-out our entire lifetime. By doing this, he has communicated that he cares enough to give up his skiing time to teach the children. The kids beam when Barry compliments them on doing well.

Do be careful in your approach to sharing talents with your children. If you aren't excited about sharing with your child, don't. You could easily discourage him if you act bored or upset during his early learning stages. But if you can communicate praise and self-worth to the child, plus enthusiasm for being able to work with him and that overall feeling that there is nothing you would rather be doing, then go to it! You and your child are on your way to enjoying an experience which few parents and children ever share.

Another aspect of communication is the sharing of spiritual experiences. This area is often neglected because spiritual moments are very personal. But I'll always remember the advice of a wise mother who told me, "Share your spiritual experiences with your children so that they might know of your inner source of strength and growth."

Also, when one of your children has a spiritual experience in his life, remind him of that moment when he's discouraged. These recollections can be a great source of strength to him.

When our oldest son started school, he found it difficult to be assertive and to speak out, even when he should have. Sometimes I became overly concerned, but Barry always put things in the right perspective. "I used to be just like him. He'll be okay," he would reassure me.

During the years since then, we have watched our shy son grow into a fine young boy. He is sensitive and alert to those ideas which he knows are right. No, he's not perfect, but he's learning and he has the potential of becoming a great man.

Once he was asked to give a five-minute talk in sacrament meeting as part of the Primary presentation. When the Primary president asked him, he didn't have the courage to say no, yet he felt deep inside that he wouldn't give it. Barry and I talked about it and weighed the consequences heavily. We knew he was scared to death of public speaking, but at the same time, we knew he had accepted an assignment. We felt he needed to learn dependability. Three weeks before the program Barry sat down with Jeff and got out the Doctrine and Covenants. He told Jeff a story from his own childhood — how he had broken his grandmother's stained-glass window and the consequences he had to pay. In fact, he told the story while all the kids were present and they giggled and wanted to hear more about their daddy as a boy. Then Barry turned to a scripture about obedience. "Why not end your talk with how you saved and saved to buy your new bike. Tell about the decision you had to make when it came time for tithing settlement. You could use the money for your bike or obey the commandment of tithing and save more for your bike. Tell how you chose the law of obedience and how the Lord blessed you for your faithfulness — you went to the store two days later and found the bike you wanted on sale."

All the family agreed that Jeff had a great talk in mind. Every night Barry listened attentively while Jeff gave his talk to the family. Before long Jeff had it completely memorized.

The Sunday of the program arrived. Jeff gave his talk once more to all of us. With fatherly concern, Barry patted Jeff on the back and said he was surely proud of him. We arrived at the church early and Jeff took a place on the stand. One of his friends called out to him: "Ha, Ha! Jeff has to give a talk."

That's all it took. With tears stinging his eyes, he quietly walked off and motioned me to follow. I felt Barry's heart sink. My heart pounded with anxiety. When I took him into a little side room, his tears started to flow. "I can't do it," he said, shaking. "I just can't do it."

"Oh, yes you can," I told him as I put my arms around him. "You just need some help. Let's get on our knees and ask Heavenly Father to help you. I know he will!"

We knelt in prayer. Through tears we asked for divine help. The prayer seemed to calm Jeff somewhat, so we went back into the chapel. Meeting had not quite started.

After the sacrament was passed, Jeff turned around. He slowly arose from his seat on the front row and headed down the aisle. Again he motioned for help. I slipped out of my seat and followed him into the hall. He disappeared into a room and I followed. He stood there sobbing. "Heavenly Father hasn't helped me yet, Mom," he cried. "There's no way I can do it. I feel like I am going to throw up."

"Maybe we need to ask him again. Let's try once more," I suggested. So again we knelt and pleaded for help.

"Oh, Mom! I'll have to cut some of my talk. Okay?" he asked, as I wiped away the tears. I don't believe in paying kids money to do an assignment and I don't know why I bribed him, but I blurted out: "Sure, and I'll even give you three dollars for getting out there and doing your best. You can use it for the pogo stick you want."

We entered the chapel just as the program started, and Jeff took his place on the stand. Barry, who sat in the audience beside me, looked sick. "How's Jeff?" he whispered. "I'm as upset as if I were giving the talk. Do you think he'll make it?"

I squeezed his hand but didn't dare speak because I was so emotional inside.

Finally Jeff stood up to speak. The entire audience became absolutely quiet. Not one baby cried. No one was whispering. Every eye was on Jeff. He looked out over the audience and started, "My talk is on obedience and I'd like to tell a story about my dad."

He went through his entire talk without cutting one line. The whole audience seemed to grasp every word. Barry was sitting there almost breathless and I fought to hold back the tears.

When the meeting was over, we noticed all of Jeff's friends patting him on the back. Adults and children alike were telling him what a great talk he had given. Barry hugged Jeff tightly. Jeff knew he had made his father feel proud.

That evening Jeff came to me and said: "You remember the three dollars you promised me? Well, I really don't want them. I just needed them to help me forget how scared I was. The minute I stood to talk, I got a good feeling all over me and I wasn't scared anymore. Heavenly Father did help me just like you said he would. And when there was no noise and everyone was listening to me, I couldn't leave out half of my story, so I told the whole thing."

We must have talked together for an hour. We talked about how the Lord does help us. I told Jeff how frightened his father was for him and how sick my stomach felt.

Jeff thanked his father for helping him with his talk. I knew that Jeff had learned many great lessons that day. As parents, Barry and I had also learned. This experience reaffirmed our convictions that we must work to prepare our children, support them in their endeavors, and pray with them for help and guidance. If we do all we can, we know the Lord will intervene at the proper time and deliver the deserved blessings.

Cinch Those Family Ties

Too many times in our families we, as parents, get so caught up in daily activities that we forget those who gave us life. Grandparents should be part of a child's growing-up experience. If you are fortunate to have grandparents living near, make sure that your children spend some time with them. Do nice things for them. Bake a special surprise or have the children prepare a little program for them. Involve the children in any thoughtful gesture you do for your parents and you will be giving your children the opportunity to build a special relationship with very special people.

Remind the children to send birthday cards to grandparents who live far away. Deliver the cards in person to grandparents who live close. I think the most special cards our children gave to their grandparents were those which they made themselves. Get out the colored paper, glue, and crayons and let the children go to work.

A mother shared this letter written by her young son for his grandpa's birthday.

Brian
Dear
Gran
Dpa

> I ho
> pe you
> have
> a nice
> birth
> day.

She continued: "It took three pages just to write it! But I know one Grandpa who surely knows he's loved."

This same mother related another story about grandchild-grandparent relationships. "A few years ago we were planning a vacation to visit my parents who were on a mission. Just before we left, Jimmy offered a little prayer in which he said: 'Thank thee that we can see Grandma and Grandpa. Thank thee that they will hug us and kiss us.' I really feel that it's the parents' responsibility to keep this love alive between the kids and their grandparents — especially when great distances are between them."

In the chapter on anticipation I mentioned how we had planned and anticipated the family trip to Disneyland. But I saved the added dimension for this chapter. Barry's folks had never been to Disneyland, and when we talked about going we could sense that they wished they were going also. Dad had bought a trailer and a Suburban van to pull the trailer and had offered to let us use them for the trip. So we told them we'd love to take the Suburban and trailer if they would come along too.

Together our three-generation family saw Disneyland for the first time! Mom and Dad got as excited over the rides as the kids did. We didn't schedule our activities because we knew that when it came time for dinner and sleeping, we could find some place to park the trailer. Barry and the kids and I stayed in the trailer at nights, and Mom and Dad slept in the Suburban.

Now as we look at our photographs of that trip, we recall many special moments. But the greatest asset of all is the memory our children have of taking the trip with their grandparents.

Every summer we anticipate our fishing trips to Idaho. My Dad and Mom have a boat and a fifth-wheeler which they keep at a campsite there. We pack our car with fishing poles, lots of good food, warm blankets and coats, and head to the campsite to go fishing. The year we camped out in our tent instead of renting a cabin is a fond memory for our children. Every year seems to bring a new experience.

For example, when Scotty was only two, he became ill in the middle of the night, and Barry had to tramp through brush and trees to get some medicine from Mom. Each year we take snapshots and motion pictures of our experiences fishing and camping. When our children grow older, they can't help but recall the evenings spent in the mountains sitting around the campfire with their grandpa and grandma and roasting marshmallows.

Not only is it comforting to know we can call upon the Lord, but there is a certain security in knowing that we do not have to raise our families alone. Even the single parent who must pray alone needs to remember that the Lord will help and sustain the family if we are diligent in asking for his help. Many families with two parents who are not united in spirituality might fall into the single parent category when it comes to communicating spiritual needs. Divine help is a necessity.

When Barry calls the family together for family prayer, when he conducts our family home evening, and when he gives advice to our family, he is communicating the patriarchal order that should be established in the home if at all possible. He is truly the head of our home and we look to him for guidance. He shows me utmost respect and thus communicates the way he wants his sons to treat their wives. He takes the time to talk to the children when he feels it necessary to discipline them. He always lets them know why they were punished.

In teaching principles of the gospel, Barry expects a great deal from the children. He expects them to attend meetings, to be reverent, to be attentive to their teachers, and to be dependable in their callings. But he expects no more from them than what he is willing to do himself. Therefore, he doesn't criticize the ward or Church leaders. He attends his meetings faithfully and never complains about going. Through example, he is teaching his family the gospel.

I relish the family home evenings when we as a family sit in front of the fire and listen to Barry read from the Book of Mormon. He inspires me to be a wife worthy of his actions and he inspires our children to be righteous individuals.

Another way we can build the grandparent-grandchild relationship is to relate stories about when we were young. Our children love to hear about the time their dad disobeyed his father and kept throwing a tennis ball against a brick wall directly above a big stained-glass window. He was told by his father to stop throwing the ball, but he kept right on. When their dad tells how the ball went crashing through the window, our children seem to sense just how their dad felt. Of course, they are always eager to hear how Grandpa made Dad work for enough money to replace the window. They like to know that their parents have been down the same road as they are traveling.

By relating stories such as this to your children, you will have a perfect opportunity to teach a moral. Barry always reminds the kids that if he had obeyed his father, he would not have broken the window.

One huge responsibility we have as parents is to speak respectfully of each other's family. When two families come together, there are certain to be differences and conflicts. But our children are grandchildren of both sets of grandparents, and if one parent starts cutting down his mate's family, only problems result. If something must be said, parents should discuss it privately, not openly where the children can hear. If a child loves his grandparents, but hears his parents talking disrespectfully about them, he will be frustrated.

Grandparents are *people* also, and they are equipped with feelings just as acute as anyone else's. Grandparents can sense when they are welcome in their children's homes and that the grandchildren delight in their visits. This is truly a wonderful gift to give grandparents.

When I read articles telling young married couples to disregard their parents' advice because parents only meddle and cause problems, I feel this counsel is unjust.

When Barry and I were first married, we wanted to be independent. I was teaching school and Barry was finishing his college education. I sometimes felt his mother was taking pity on us because she invited us over for Sunday dinner every week. So one time I said I didn't want to go. His mom was really hurt. She knew that our finances were limited and that I was swamped preparing my lesson plans. She was limited in ways to help us, but she felt that inviting us to dinner might be one small way of making our burdens lighter. Instead of being wise and understanding, I was defensive and headstrong. I'm sure that many times Barry's folks felt like "throwing in the towel." But they cared for us and therefore swallowed their pride and continued to treat me kindly.

When we had our first baby, my mother was ecstatic, for he was also her first grandchild. I'll never forget her first visit — she had more presents than I had ever seen at Christmas! Barry nearly died! He took me into a room and said: "Your mom doesn't have to buy the baby everything. I can take care of my family."

I recalled my own response to his mother's well-intended gestures, and I shared with him what I had learned. "Jeff is our son," I said, "but he is also our parents' grandchild, and the first one at that. Let Mom have her joy in giving to someone whom she is so delighted to have come into the family."

I guess parents have to be careful not to imply that they doubt their children's ability to succeed alone when they get married. But we, as children, have a responsibility to weigh the actions of our parents and not be so quick to judge. Usually their advice is given because of their love and concern. They don't want us to make the same mistakes they did. Sometimes we would be much further ahead if we listened more.

Since I was raised in a rural area, our diet was simple: meat, potatoes, and milk. I had a sweet tooth and thought that when I was on my own, I would always have something sweet in the house. And that I did. The problem came when we had children. Since there was pop in the fridge, candy in the cupboard, and cookies in a jar, our children acquired a sweet tooth also. My dad was really upset.

"Karla," he told me, "you are going to ruin your children.

There are very few things you can give your children which are more important than a healthy body. You had better watch what they are eating!"

Wow! I was really upset. But luckily I didn't blow off steam. When I was all alone, I contemplated Dad's advice. I hated to admit it, but I *was* wrong. I was letting the kids eat too much candy and pop. Now as I look back, I'm glad my dad didn't stand back and let me do my own thing. He said what he did because he loves his grandchildren and he wants the best for them.

Go to your parents for advice. They have traveled the way before and they have learned through experience some of the pitfalls. Maybe we have our advanced degrees in education, but sometimes we overlook the education gained through experience. We need to respect the knowledge and inspiration which our parents previously learned.

The other day I was talking with a wise grandmother who offered these ideas: "When I see parents pushed aside and put into nursing homes and never visited, I think of all the wasted knowledge. If young people would seek counsel and take advice from those who love them and want the best for them, they would avoid making many terrible mistakes. But young people are advised to move away from the 'old folks' and to do their own thing. I have learned many things while raising my family and being a wife. I don't want my children to make the same mistakes I did. I want them to have a better life than I have had. And I want my grandchildren to have even a better life than their parents. I am so thankful our children come to us for advice. Out of deep love for them, we are very careful to only give ideas which can benefit them."

One way to salvage the wasted knowledge is to tape record interviews with older people. You might want to go to a nursing home for such interviews or to the homes of older friends and relatives. If you have a grandparent or relative who is old, involve your family in writing a list of questions which would be interesting to discuss with the older person. Then set up a time to visit with your relative and interview him. (Unless the children are older, however, go alone. Sometimes little ones can distract, and you won't have a very good interview.) A person's body might grow old, but many times his mind is still alert and eager to be a part of the world. Too often we only see the deteriorated body and consider the person useless.

My grandmother is my only living grandparent. Luckily, she is still healthy, can take care of herself, and likes being independent. One weekend when we went to visit my parents, I spent a great deal of time with her. I wanted to know what her life as a young girl had been. She delighted in telling me how she had loved to jump the rope (her aunt told her that she had better not jump so much or she would ruin her legs). She told of her love for horses. She told how she met Grandpa. He had come from Sweden and didn't know the English language. Grandma knew how to write and speak Swedish, and so she taught Grandpa English.

As we visited, I realized I needed to record those stories and events in her life. Our children are young and they might not have the opportunity of hearing her tell the stories to them. So I told Grandma I wanted to write her life story.

By taking on that project, I learned so much about my heritage. Comparing myself to her, I could identify some of my inherited characteristics. Knowing of her struggles and triumphs in life made me understand and love her even more.

My eyes were opened. I couldn't stop with Grandma's story. I wanted to know of my other grandparents and even of my own parents. So I scheduled an entire year and allowed two months' time for the writing of each history. The histories included my father, mother, and both sets of grandparents.

For my grandmother's story I relied on interviews with her and comments from her children. For Mom's and Dad's stories I interviewed them also. Whenever they came to visit, we spent time together talking about their early life up to the present day. At the outset, comments from both were similar: "Oh, Karla, you know all about us."

But as they shared their thoughts and philosophies, I realized how little I knew of them. Again, I grew to love and understand them more, knowing what they had passed through.

When I worked on the life stories of my grandparents who

had passed away, I had to rely on family members and friends who could supply information. I was very lucky that I had been close to my grandparents so that I could record my memories and describe my grandparents as I still saw them in my mind. It was the descriptions of how they had looked and some of the moments I had shared with them which seemed to bring them to life for our children.

December of that year came and I had finished the last life story. I made copies for my brothers, sister, Mom, Dad, and Grandmother. I have never given any gift which has brought me the joy I felt when I presented these Christmas gifts. Needless to say, each receiver was deeply touched. But it wasn't until they had read each story that they fully appreciated what was inside their binders. In fact, one brother called several months later and said he had read the stories again and wanted to thank me again for that special gift. "I had no idea about some of the things Mom and Dad felt," he said. "Reading the stories made me take mental notes on the story I could leave to my children."

If our children can see us doing projects or special things for our family members, such as family histories, we also communicate how much we care for family members. Speak kindly of each other's brothers and sisters. They are your children's aunts and uncles, and you want your children to admire and respect them. We all make mistakes. Consider the good traits (you are bound to find some) in each other's family members.

At the first of every year take a calendar and note throughout the year all of the birthdays of grandparents, aunts, uncles, and cousins. At the first of each month check to see whose birthday is upcoming and, if nothing more, take time on their birthday to telephone and wish them happy birthday. On my last birthday throughout the entire evening I enjoyed long-distance phone calls from my brothers, sister, and parents. What a warm feeling I had knowing that they remembered my birthday and took the time to call.

So take advantage of the telephone or post office to keep in touch with your loved ones on special occasions. Such little things will keep you together as a family, although you might be hundreds of miles apart.

Use names of endearment for each other's parents. When Barry and I got married, I couldn't call his parents Mom and Dad. I was very close to my parents and I felt I would be disloyal to them if I used the same name for others. So I always talked right to Barry's parents instead of addressing them first.

When my brother got married, I noticed how his wife called my folks Mom and Dad. I noticed how pleased my parents looked when addressed by her. So I took my mother aside and asked her if she liked her new daughter-in-law to call her Mom.

"Oh, yes," she confided. "That makes me feel like she wants to be a real part of the family and I know it pleases your father."

The next time I was around Barry's folks, I felt myself almost rehearsing what I would say. The first time I sputtered out "Mom," I know I sounded nervous. But the second time came easier and the third even easier. I noticed that one time when I called Barry's father Dad he got such a pleasant look on his face. By adding those two words in my conversation with them, I broke down a barrier. They even found it easier to call me something other than Karla.

Being called aunt or uncle by a niece or nephew is also a name of endearment. So when talking about your brothers or sisters with the children, refer to them as Aunt Suzy or Uncle Larry. Then the children will get into the habit of addressing their aunts and uncles properly.

Tell your children stories about your childhood — the things you did with your brothers and sisters. Tell them everyday-type stories that they can relate to.

Barry and I have a strong desire to help build a bond among our own children. One story which helps to put this point across is about my older brother and myself.

When growing up the boys were not allowed to slug or hit the girls. (Mother said the boys would grow up thinking they could hit their wives.) Naturally, my sister and I took advantage of the situation. Often we teased our brothers until they succumbed and were ready to start hitting back, but we'd make a quick dart to be within distance of Mother's hearing.

But one time I went too far. I had started an argument with my brother Kent, but all of a sudden he was the one teasing me. I grabbed a broom, chased him down the stairs, and hit him hard on the head. He was so infuriated that he turned around and slugged me as hard as he could in the stomach. It hurt my stomach as well as my pride. I didn't think he would ever hit me, not only because hitting wasn't allowed, but also because we were very close and I thought a lot of him. I ran upstairs to my room and slammed the door. He followed me and kept opening my door, trying to apologize for what he had done. I'll never forget the look in his big brown eyes as he said: "I'm sorry, Karla. I'll never do that again." That was the last argument I can ever remember having with my brother.

Every time I tell the story, the kids want to talk about how I felt when Kent hit me. They want to know why I teased him in the first place.

After telling experiences such as this one, I can express some very warm and positive feelings about my family. Of course, I am hoping the children will aspire to build good relationships with each other.

Weave the family ties strong within your home. By using phrases, such as, "Say goodnight to your neat sister," the children are getting reinforcement that their sister is "neat." Tell stories about family activities to jog their memories so that they'll recall the good times spent with the family.

As parents, plan special trips or activities which will become exciting memories. Do unique things on holidays and birthdays which the children will always remember. Take pictures and keep them in a family album because looking at pictures jogs the memory.

Express your feelings and let the children know you like being their parents, that you are so grateful that each of them is a part of the family. By playing, working, planning, and praying together, you can strengthen bonds which will hold you together for eternity!

Admiring Each Other

Some of the first advice which Barry and I received shortly before marriage was to avoid cutting remarks about each other in public. Even jokes which could make the spouse look ridiculous were no-nos, because usually a certain amount of hurt would develop inside the person even though he might laugh.

Share the good, instead of the bad, traits of your spouse with friends and family; you'll find yourself excited to tell how you marvelled at the way he could ski, or the way she could cook, or the way he could straighten the house. Adults thrive on praise as much as children do.

If a husband likes the way his wife cooks, fixes her hair, or works with the children, he should express this verbally. Too often if a spouse appears self-confident, the other partner feels that it is unnecessary to compliment. "She knows I like her cooking" is a common example. But unless the husband says it sometimes, the wife doesn't know his feelings — then resentment enters the wife's mind and she suspects her efforts are expected rather than appreciated.

So, husbands, if your wife cooks something you think is especially tasty, tell her. If you like the perfume she's wearing, tell her. She'll wear it more often if she knows you notice. If you like the way she keeps an orderly home, tell her. If you think her clothing is becoming, tell her. If you appreciate her stopping what she's doing to sit and talk with you, tell her. She'll talk with you more often. If you admire the way she performs a church or service job in the community, tell her. She'll do even better if she knows you are watching and admiring.

Conversely, the same is true for husbands. Wives, if your husband is good to play with the children, tell him you appreciate it. He'll take more time with them. If you admire the way he dresses, tell him. Be specific also. If he has a certain suit you like him in, tell him how great he looks when he wears it. If you like the cologne he chooses, tell him. If he calls you from work during the day, tell him you enjoy his thoughtfulness. If you like him to compliment you, tell him how much it means to you.

Too many times we imagine that our mate *knows* our innermost feelings, but too often we are wrong. Reaffirm your feelings vocally and sincerely, and you will discover you're working even harder to make each other happy.

The opposite approach — attacking and nagging — only brings on defensive actions and destroys the desire to please. As human beings we want acceptance, especially by those we love. If we feel our mates are displeased or disappointed in us, usually we lose the desire to build up our loved one. We salve our wounds by hurting the other person. Then we get into a vicious circle of "you hurt me, so I'll hurt you."

People marry for different reasons. Each man has his own ideas as to what a wife and mother should be. Each woman has her own distinct ideas about husbands. Therefore, it is very important to sit down together either before marriage or after and to make a list for each other of attributes you like.

Right before we were married, I made a list of things I liked about Barry:

1. You always look so neat and clean, as if you just got out of the shower.
2. You wear good-looking clothes.
3. You are handsome and have a great build.
4. Everyone else thinks you are neat.
5. You always ask me for a date in advance.

6. You have many qualities which could lead to conceit, yet you are unaffected.
7. You are so interesting! You can ski, play the guitar, swim well, water ski and you like sports.

The list goes on to number 14, but I think you've got the idea. Compare this list to the one I gave to Barry after we had been married for six months.

1. You are so understanding about women's problems.
2. You consider my wants and wishes.
3. You try so hard to please me.
4. You help me with the housework.
5. You are patient.
6. You already have ideas about raising children.
7. You make life worthwhile and mean everything to me.

Note how the "important things" changed in just a few months. Both men and women change in their thinking of what is most important; that is why it is vital to share your ideas with your mate. Tell each other your innermost feelings and share your expectations and dreams.

As I look over the love letters and notes which I sent to Barry before we were married, I marvel at how hard I tried to convey my love to him. I made him chocolate fudge and put it in his car so he'd find it when he came out of his college class. I left notes wishing him a good day and good luck on a test. I took the time to listen to him talk about his dreams. I always made sure I looked my best when he saw me, and I was eager to experiment with a new perfume to try and please him. I found clever cards to send to him, just to let him know I was thinking of him. I was gracious to his friends, because I wanted them to feel that Barry was getting a good wife. If at all possible, I arranged my appointments and obligations around time with Barry.

Why, if I did only half of those things now, twelve years later, our marriage would *have* to sparkle! Too often we forget how hard we tried to win each other's love and once we have framed the marriage certificate, our efforts begin to slow down.

I recall one day when Barry wore his grey suit, I happened to stop and take special notice. I had often thought how handsome he was in that suit, but this time I took the time to tell him how I felt. His eyes lit up and I could sense he was pleased at my comments. (Inwardly, I feel ten years younger whenever he takes time to compliment me on my appearance, so why wouldn't he feel younger too?) All of a sudden I felt more like a sweetheart than a wife, and sometimes a woman needs to reexperience that.

No matter how many years you have been married, sit down together and make a list of what you like about each other. Work on the positive side and try to list some of the little things you both like. Many times when we are working to make someone else happy, most of the negative things seem to slip right out of the picture. Be honest with each other. If there is something about your relationship which has been bothering you, don't keep it inside any longer. Tell your mate that you must talk out a problem. By approaching your mate with how badly you feel or how hurt you are inside, you will not bring on defensive actions. Generally the misunderstanding can be solved when you both express your honest feelings and your reasons for those feelings.

Instead of saying, "You are so insensitive to my problems . . . ," try the approach, "I am really hurting because . . ."

In our society today the idea that a man and a woman each has a specific role is almost taboo. We are encouraged to let the husband clean the house and let the wife earn a living. But what's wrong with having a specific role?

When a student accepts his role of being a student and his teacher functions in the role of teacher, the classroom usually runs quite smoothly. But try mixing up those roles — chaos results. Chaos can similarly result between husband and wife when they do not understand their roles or function in them.

Current articles encourage women to step out of the role of housewife if they want to be fulfilled. Leave the diapers, washing, and cooking. Put on a new outfit and find employment which fulfills your needs. The idea is often presented in a way which sounds intriguing and adventurous so as to lure mothers out of homes.

There is nothing wrong with being a wife and homemaker. In

fact, a wife can discover much fulfillment and contentment in the role of caring for her husband, children, and home. Few joys exceed seeing a son, daughter, or husband achieve success, especially when you, the wife and mother, played a large part in that success.

One woman worked in her profession for four years and then stayed home to raise a family. She acknowledged the fact that the rewards of being a mother were slower in coming than the fleeting rewards of being a professional. "But I have never found a greater joy than seeing the progress of my children and knowing that I am responsible in part. At first I missed the pats on the back and the awards. But compared to what I have now achieved, that all seems superficial."

I grew up in a role-oriented environment. While the men worked hard in the fields, the women worked hard in the homes. Each was respected for the work he did and each realized the need for the other.

When I moved to the city and married a certified public accountant, I wondered if the roles would be extremely different. Since there were no children involved at first, I also went the professional route. I learned that every day is not always perfect and that if I wanted success, I had to work for it. I enjoyed success and I discovered for myself that I could be quite independent. But that wasn't enough! I didn't have the time to do little things for Barry to spark up his day. I was always concerned about the things *I* needed to do for *my* work. Our marriage was just fine, but the sparkle was missing.

Then I became a mother and stayed at home. At first I missed the hectic working life. I missed the feeling of being a part of the world "out there." But a whole new world of discoveries was awaiting me. The role of being a wife and mother was most exciting. Never had I had such a wide scope of freedom to try out my creative prowess. I didn't care for the menial tasks such as dusting and vacuuming, so I hurried through them early in the morning.

My days were mine. I had the time to do little things for Barry and the children. From experience I knew what the working field was like, and I wanted Barry to always be thankful he could come home after a long day at the office. So Barry earned the money to buy the food I cooked, I stayed home, and the sparkle began to return to our marriage. I knew he was proud of what I did as a wife and mother, and he knew I was proud of his success in his profession.

Oh, yes, we do slip into each other's role occasionally. When I get behind in my housework, Barry lends me a hand. When Barry needs some typing done or help with his work, I enjoy going to his aid. But we have our roles, we feel successful in them, and we feel the joy of working together. Like the various motor parts which combine their individual roles to make the automobile go, we function smoothly when we work together.

Make your spouse your "best friend." This will involve doing things for him or her which you might do for a good friend. Husband, take your wife to lunch. Wife, bake his favorite pie or cake and write "I Love You" on the top. Instead of always going out with a group, go out with each other and enjoy a pleasant evening. Instead of telling a friend your exciting news, share it first with your spouse. When you need advice, ask your mate for an opinion and then respect that advice.

Keep your family business at home and never, *never* talk to other people about each other or your problems and dis-agreements. Any problems should be settled privately between the two of you. Few things destroy faith in a marriage quicker than discovering that your private matters are not private.

Someone once told me that the reason a person doesn't find fulfillment in the role of either a husband or a wife is that he or she is not willing to go the "second mile."

Remember the kind words and actions you employed to win each other years ago. It's amazing what fresh flowers can do for a wife and what a backrub can do for a husband.

In doing the extras and making your marriage exciting, not only will each of you find great joy and happiness, but you will also be setting examples for the kind of husbands and wives your children will become. When a mom and dad love each other and enjoy each other's company, the children sense the peace and contentment. They are secure in knowing that peace can exist. What a gift you are giving them in a world of discontent, hatred, and wars!

But in order to achieve this peace, constant effort, thought, and planning are required. Start on the "second mile" today. Remember the things which make your spouse's eyes sparkle and then start doing those things. Instead of wondering *if* your marriage will work, use your brain and heart to concoct ideas which will *make* your marriage work!

No One Says It's Easy

While reading this book you must remember that Barry and I are still struggling as parents. For every answer we have found, there is another problem for which we need another answer. I'm sure that you've not found the answers to all of your problems in this book. But let me share one important thing we've learned. As we observe good families and good parents of those families, we try to find an opportunity to ask them for advice. What pitfalls should we be watching for? Are certain antics that our children try normal? How are the channels of communication kept open through the teenage years? How do parents incorporate and encourage the study of good and uplifting material in their home? There are so many things we need to know. When we've asked for advice, many good parents have given us great ideas which we now use to make our family better.

Every time I have asked admirable mothers what advice they could give me concerning young children, they have *always* cautioned me to spend as much time as possible with my little ones because the time goes so quickly.

When you, as young mothers, are overburdened with diapers and formula and household chores, it is easy to panic and to wonder if things will ever be different. To those mothers who are right in the middle of this quandary, let me assure you that the years do go quickly. It seems only yesterday that all three babies needed my constant attention. Now we have three little people who can put on their own coats, prepare their own snacks, get their own drinks of water, and clean up their own messes. But thank heaven for the wise mothers who told me to take time with my little ones. Had I not learned to crawl on the floor with them, or invite myself into their worlds, I know that I would not be having as much fun with them as I do now. A relationship with your children does not begin after the diapers and formula have ended. Somehow you have to start that very day when they seem to call to you in the delivery room.

Learn to confide in your parents. If you are as lucky as Barry and I in having good parents, you have a wealth of information within your grasp. When couples first get married they want to strike out on their own; I don't know what it is inside of us that makes us want to prove to the entire world that we can do this alone. We don't need any advice from those who raised us because we are going to change the world and be super intelligent parents. But when Barry and I looked around and saw the good brothers and sisters which we have, we knew our parents must have been wise in raising us.

Raising a family is an awesome responsibility. With each new child and each new year of growth, new problems arise. It is easy to see only the problems and to feel overwhelmed. But there is so much good that can come from being a family; the effort is a small price to pay.

One of the mottos which has helped our family is "Treat your children and spouse like your best friends."

One evening I had a speaking engagement. As I stood at the podium, I looked down into the faces of my four best friends. They didn't say a word, but every one of their expressions told me that I had four fans who wanted me to succeed. No matter what I've tried, whether I failed or won, they have supported me to the utmost.

I think of the fall when our son became a Cub Scout and he entered the Pine Wood Derby. His father was swamped with his work, but he worked late into the night helping Jeff build a race car. As they painted and did the final touches, every one of us was there with our "oohs" and "ahhs." Jeff didn't have to ask us to support him. He knew that he had four fans who would cheer for him no matter what happened. As his little car raced down the track, every one of our faces was flushed with excitement. Even when the "Dallas Dart" didn't come in first, we were still cheering for it. But what an exciting moment in our lives when Jeff won a trophy for the design of his car. You would have thought the Ericksons had won the Grand Prix!

In building our friendships, we have all had to learn a lot of lessons. I had to learn to apologize when I was wrong. At first it was difficult for me to apologize to the children, because I was the parent and I didn't want to have to admit that I had made a mistake. But by my learning to apologize, the children could see that if they too erred, they needed to amend the situation.

We had to learn to keep alive our manners. I learned to enjoy thanking my family for helping me. When I showed them respect, they returned the kindness. They continue to like the feeling of all of us being friends.

But there always come those instances when Barry and I have to discipline or say no. We explain our reasons to them, but hold firm to our convictions. We realize that we do not know all the answers and maybe some of our judgments are wrong. But we know that if we act out of love for the child, we cannot be too far from what is right. Knowing how or when to discipline the children is one of the hardest parts of being a parent. I recall telling Barry that being a mother would be so much easier if I didn't have to discipline.

Not a day goes by that we don't pray for guidance in raising our children. We chose to be parents and to assume the responsibilities involved. We feel the need for divine help. We want to do those things which will help our children grow up to be secure and responsible individuals who also want the responsibilities and joys of parenthood. We know our dreams are set high and that the only way we can achieve them is to have help from the Lord.

Take the time to pray for help. Take the time to be perceptive parents. Be aware of the things which count. An encouraging

word, a thoughtful gesture, and a look of concern and understanding are the gifts in life our children need.

Time is elusive. It gets away from us fast. But if it is used
wisely, time can be one of the greatest gifts which God gives
parents.